Union Island "Caribbean Paradise" Then and Now

Copyright © 2012 by Joseph Stewart
Published by Josiah Stewart First Edition 2014
Front cover photograph by Josiah Stewart
Josiah Stewart (718) 532-6334
Book Interior and Cover designed by George M. Rodrigues (Café Urban)
Library of Congress Txu 1-797-154

ISBN 9780991337408

If you have been asked, who were Joseph Chateau, DuValle, and Captain Hugh Mulzac and your response is "Who?" know that you are not alone. Clearly there are a number of factors that contribute to your lack of knowledge within that realm. Being unaware is not completely your fault, mind you! As the author indicated in *The Impetus*, "The historical stem wall was never set in place for the promulgation of regional history, much less a 3.5 sq. mile landmass called Union Island." Evidently, the onus of responsibility to publicize our history and her-story now lies squarely on our shoulders. It is a solemn duty we now owe to our ancestors and our children. We MUST disseminate now to the masses of our people, the irrefutable truth, fact and proof of our past.

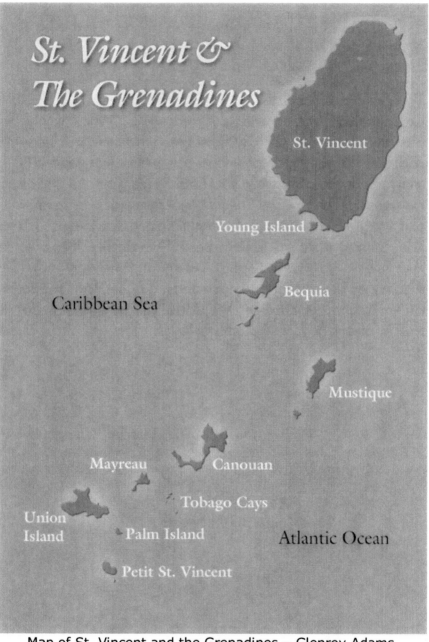

Map of St. Vincent and the Grenadines – Glenroy Adams

ENJOY THE ADVENTURE
Josiah Stewart Sr.

Union Island

CARIBBEAN PARADISE

Then & Now

* * *

Part 1

You are about to embark on an exciting journey.

An insight
To understanding the journey of the ancestors and
the shaping of the island's culture.

DEDICATION

To Union Island with Love

Also

To my brother Urias Augustin Stewart (08-31-1959) to (06-19-1989), Herbert Israel Thomas (12-30-1961) to (08-12-2013), my friend, and Agatha Andrews (04-30-1955) to (04-19-1996), the beloved mother of my daughter Shaniah. Your transitions have shaken my foundation, but have enlightened me considerably about life's brevity.

May your rests be long, but placid.

Table of Contents

Foreword

Helping to put this book together was not an easy task.

However, it did teach me the rich history of Union Island and of the struggles the people faced together. Taking steps back in time to relive my father's childhood; his perspective of the world in his earlier years, showed me how oblivious I was as a child of immigrants. The daily challenges prior to setting foot abroad are being brought to light here in *Union Island Then & Now*. It is further compelling as it combines history, personal strife and economic concerns for the reader to arrive at his/her own conclusion of the future of the island. I believe that this book can lend a hand and be of great use when utilized in an academic setting. The history of Union Island is in many ways the history of the rest of the Caribbean; just perhaps occurring in a different order.

It is very important to realize that each island has its own jargon, culture, and history that resulted in how it is today. It was a pleasure working on this book and hopefully it enhances your take on the Caribbean Diaspora as beyond only a series of island chains that advertise sand, sea, and sun to those who are not natives.

Shaniah Stewart.

Acknowledgements

To my dear friend Pamela Grant, and my editor-in-chief, Shaniah Stewart for bringing my work to a point where the reader can now assume command. I owe a debt of gratitude to you both. I am happy to be surrounded by enthusiastic individuals who have rendered support to me throughout my tedious journey on this book. They saw something remarkable in me and were very eager to see that my literary work come to fruition. Among them, are Sheila, Khalid, Khadijah, Niael, Evelyn Lucas, Herbert Thomas, Andy Stewart, Ricky Wilson, Joy DesVignes, and Valerie. To my classmates of Swedish Institute who are always energized to hear me speak passionately about Union Island, an island that they have never heard of before. On campus, we worked hard and stayed together throughout the entire course. They are: Adriana Almanzar, Tinean Livingston, Cassandra Fleurimond, Ann Marie Turner, Cindy Rodriguez, Mallorie Guevarez, Naiyma Livingston, Gabriel Poonce and Alice Lock. To my instructors: Ms. Shoba Parasram, Cindya Coffey, Hazel Bernardino, Giselle Peralta, Dr. Sherman, Dr. Nihad Atlic, Dr. Fredric Cohen, Dr. Jeremy Moss, Raul Castillo, Juan Pilarte, and Mr. Scott Freer. Your vast knowledge has permanently transformed our lives; fortunately we cannot return to our former selves. To you guys I am very thankful. I love you all.

Special appreciation goes to the following individuals who gave freely of their time and energy to help make *Union Island Then & Now* a reality as well. Among this invaluable group are: Mr. Mills McIntosh, Augustus "King" Mitchell, Minister Leroy Thomas, Jenny Charles, Norma, Tyler, Kay Thomas, Junior Coy, Leonard Scrubb, Carlton Stewart, Maria Alexander, Annette & Stephen Thomas, Lorette & Godwin James, Junior Polson, Holden Regis, Keith Stewart, Carolyn Stewart, Millicent Alcide (Liz), Marjorie Roache, John Thomas and most importantly, the ever-present Sheila Stewart who never ceases to amaze me. From those who are now deceased, their information remains priceless.

They are: Charles "Mindo" Stewart, Mr. Alfred Cox, Ms. Mappish, Ce Julie, Janey Stewart, Janey Roache, Ethneil Mitchell,

Telina Roache, and my dad Garfield Stewart. I also owe an incredible amount of appreciation to my great granny Isabella Roache, the old lady who evoked the never-ending historical passion of Union Island in me. For their contributions, I owe a tremendous amount of gratitude and priceless thankfulness.

Special recognition again goes to my daughter Shaniah, who has been my inspiration since her birth in 1994, and now Khalid Josiah Stewart Jr., my last son. They both have helped to put my life on an even keel during my sojourn away from my natural habitat. To Eileen Stewart, for her priceless interventions during the many demanding times of my life, I must say that I am eternally grateful.

To the many, whose names are too numerous to mention, I must say categorically that I am eternally indebted to you.

And the last word belongs to my mother Sheila E. Stewart. For all that I am and hope to be, I owe it to her indelible.

To all of you for your collective help and intervention into my space, I feel loved, honored, and greatly inspired to continue my literary work with renewed energy and cheerful readiness. Once again, I thank you.

AUTHOR'S NOTE

After meticulously studying and analyzing the history of the people of Union Island, I observed that there is a trend that was born during the early 20th century. This inexorable trend has resulted from the sharecropping era, which superseded the period of slavery. Regrettably, this trend has escalated during the 1930s and has yet to show any signs of decline. Unfortunately, it is there to stay. But what is that trend, and why? Well, as the reader carefully delves deeper into the contents of *Union Island Then and Now*, it will substantially advance his/her understanding of the socioeconomic life of Union Island. He/she will be apprised of the salient factors and influences that necessitate that trend. These factors are largely responsible for the molding and shaping of the island's culture.

In a lengthy interview/discussion with the late Ethneil Mitchell on December 28, 2010, she had quite a bit to say. This noble lady was a respectable citizen, and former schoolteacher of the first government primary school on the island (still referred to as Small School). We spoke extensively, but passionately on several issues that are affecting the island as a whole. But most importantly, we deliberate on *that* trend which we believe is most impactful on the island's culture. We later deemed it as *The Exodus Factor*.

The lives of Unionites were never without challenges, but amidst those trying times, there was always laughter that derived from humor that might be unique to this little island. With that in mind, I felt obligated to incorporate that humor with real life's experiences -the type that was native to our ancestors, yet it remains as current as the air we breathe.

The tasty dialect of Union Island has always been integral to the island's culture. Hence it is sprinkled throughout this book to enhance flavor, yet evoke a feeling of homeliness. To omit this, would be a blatant act of dereliction.

Attention! For every baby boomer that has spent some part of their life on Union Island, what you read will evoke passion and emotion.

Also, relevant in this book is *The Impetus*, which is key to your understanding. It tells a bit about my experience on this little island during my formative years. It also creates a pathway to clearly understand this entire manuscript.

I believe this work; the compilation of the history and her-story of the people of Union Island in *Union Island Then & Now* should be oriented towards the classroom. It will inform, engage, excite and enlighten many on the history of our pasts, a unique one indeed.

Immerse yourselves now and enjoy the compilation of the history of the people of Union Island known as Unionites.

THE IMPETUS

Port of Spain, Trinidad, on January 1, 1968: I had just had my sixth birthday when my mother told my sister and me that we were going to Union Island to live. At six, I did not know what she meant and had never heard of Union Island. To be frank, I was so innocent that I did not know what an island was. A couple of weeks later, I learned that this beautiful little island, which is situated some 180 miles North of Trinidad, was the place of my birth. My parents told me that they had taken me to Trinidad when I was only three months old.

Two days before our departure, I dreamed of my grandmother, a woman whom I had never seen before. On January 15, 1968, we left the city of Port of Spain on a vessel named Speedy Queen bound for Union Island; water transport was the only viable means to gain access to the island. Two days later, about midday, we arrived at the small port of Clifton, Union Island. There we met with two other siblings, Urias and Ezrard. The sun was exceedingly hot, and the landscape was very flat. It was amazing to see the sandy surrounding, but I was fascinated when I saw goats and cows tied to their stakes. I had never seen that before. I thought they were close to the road and wanted to touch them. That day I saw my grandmother, Telina Roache, for the first time. Her head was wrapped in a red bandana, which she called a head-tie, and her face was a replica of the person I had dreamed about a few nights earlier. I later learned that the bandana that Grandma had wrapped around her head was one of the customs of the female slaves on the plantations of Union Island. They were given head scarfs by the slave masters, and commanded to keep their head tied at all time; because the slave master thought that the hairs of most female slaves on the plantations were disheveled. Grandma took us from the jetty at Clifton Harbor and walked us all the way to Point Lookout to meet my great-grandmother, Isabella Roache.

In the community, everyone calls Isabella Ta Muggy, but we call her "Ma." Grandma took us into the little house to greet Ma, and then a few minutes later she went approximately two hundred feet away to her own little house. Ma held me and kissed me, then later seated me on a wooden bench. I could have touched the other side of the house; it was that small.

I remember seeing a bee trapped in her curtain, and as I rose to catch it, I was stung and in pain. Almost instantly, my index finger began to swell. Immediately I placed my hands on my head and screamed as loud as I can. Ma looked at me and shouted, "Take yo hands off yo head; yo want to kill yo modder?" With tears in my eyes, I stared at the woman, and suddenly she came to my rescue. She tore a piece of cloth from an old dress that she had, and with some Canadian healing oil, she dressed and tied my little finger firmly. "Felix, don't worry," she exclaimed in a gentle voice. She then opened a jar of paradise plums and Kaiser balls (candies), and with a soft smile, she placed one of those huge candies into my mouth. Instantly I smiled, but was quite baffled; I did not understand what she meant when she asked if I wanted to kill my mother. A few years later, I learned that she was referring to one of the superstitious beliefs that are native to Union Island. According to the superstition, if any youngster put his/her hands on their head, their mother will die soon after.

I stared at my great-granny while observing the distinct difference in her dialect but remained intensively perceptive to everything she had to say.

She proceeded to place me on her lap to assuage the pain of my swollen finger. It was during my short stay on her lap that I received my first lesson on the history of Union Island. Ma told me about a slave on a Union Island plantation that refused to work and was subsequently buried alive. She also referred to another who had the roof of his house yanked off; as she told the story, she pointed in the direction where his little shack was situated. She mentioned that she already had a daughter named Clouden and a son named James when the incident had happened. My granny also told me about her years as a child growing up in Clifton; about her involvement in the Maroon Festival (described in another chapter), the Big Drum Dance, catching turtles, picking salt, and doing other activities on the island. She said to me in a gentle voice, "Boy when you get bigger, you will bring me some turtle eggs and crabs, yo hear?"

Although I did not understand fully what she was saying, I smiled and nodded affirmatively. I guess that's what she expected me to do. One thing for sure, I remembered most of her words vividly.

Seeing how attentive I was, my mother, Sheila, laughed when she mentioned the Maroon, and she teased the old lady about her dancing during the festivals. "You always jump and hold your frock during the Maroon Dance." Mom exclaimed. "Less yo noise Sheila," Ma retorted. "What you know about Maroon dance? You don't know that I was one ah the best dancers in Clifton?" Mom burst out in laughter. Before we could settle on who was right, we left Point Lookout for Campbell, a small district of Union Island where my parents had a small wooden house. We settled in nicely, and that became our home for the next twelve years.

At Campbell, I observed that the houses were situated far apart from each other, and at Point Lookout it was the same. My grandfather, Charles Stephen Stewart, also had a small house there; the neighbors called him Ba Mindo, but all of his grandchildren call him Dada. He had loved me very much; one afternoon, he looked at me and said to my father Garfield, "Gaf, this is one of us." He meant that I resembled his side of the family very much, and he was pleased about it. Amazingly, thirty-four years later in Brooklyn, New York, my father looked at one of my daughters and said to me, "Felix, this is one of us." I was speechless, but we had a hearty laugh. I think the onus might be on me now to perpetuate that legacy. I guess it's a Stewart thing.

Meanwhile, my sister Lyris and I were bored to death in that little district of Campbell because we did not get to watch TV or play with other children. Urias and Ezrard had already adjusted to the way of life in Union Island, having lived there since six months prior to our arrival. The nights at Campbell were very dark, but the darkness was driven away by the kerosene lamp, which was our only source of light. I can still vividly remember our first lampshade, with the words "Home Sweet Home" on it before Lyris caused it to fall and break. That happened on a late Friday evening, and that night our little lamp remained lit without a shade.

Days at Campbell turned into weeks, and weeks into months, but eventually we were able to cope in our new environment. Then suddenly we lost our grandfather who died.

He was 84 years old.

It was on a Thursday afternoon, April 25, 1968; my mother was attending a meeting at her church. My siblings and I were all alone at home when my brother Urias and I decided to pay Dada a visit. It was approximately 4:00 P.M. We went right into the old man's house, for his doors were never locked. Urias trotted straight into his bedroom, but I remained in the living room. It wasn't even a minute when Urias ran back out of the bedroom and quietly whispered to me, "Come, ah think Dada dead." I was unmoved. Then immediately, we went into our grandfather's bedroom and there, the old man, was, lying motionlessly. My brother was right; the old man was dead indeed. That night so many people came by to pay their respects, I thought I saw the entire village of Ashton at his home. Most women in attendance had their head nicely tied with heads ties. In the huge crowd, an old lady gazed at me and said to her husband, "O gad, this little boy favor Garfield eh?" (O my God, this little boy resembles Garfield, don't you think?) Later during the night, my mother put a plate of water with Trumpet grass on the dead man's chest. It is believed that Trumpet grass with the water prohibits the belly of the dead from rising.

The following day, hundreds of relatives, friends, and well wishers converged to pay their last respects at the Ashton Cemetery. He was laid to rest at 5:07 P.M.

Immediately after the burial, my brother and I slowly walked up to the main road; there we met our great aunt, Liz (Elizabeth Simmons). Aunty Liz was crying hysterically and yelling, "Me wan, me wan." She meant that all of her brothers and sisters had died, and she was the only one still alive. With so many people crying around us, and without a teardrop coming from our eyes, we felt out of place. I held the head of my brother and said to him quietly, "I think we supposed to cry too." He looked at me as though he was pondering but never responded.

My sister and I had been taken out of Piccadilly Government School in Trinidad, and we needed to resume our school in Union Island. Early that year, I was enrolled at the Ashton Primary School, referred to as "Small School." Lyris and Urias were inrolled at another primary school. Amazingly, during my first school term, I saw two students with writing slates in the classroom, but never seen one since. Unfortunate for us, our teachers were senior students who had just left school after receiving a certificate; they were only 15 years old. This issue of having inexperienced teenagers as educators during my formative years will be expanded in another book. Unluckily, I never was able to assimilate fully into the entire school system of Union Island.

My mother then bought me The West Indian Reader. It was the sole textbook used at the school, and we committed to memorizing many parts of this book rather than comprehending them. In retrospect, many past students will agree that the content of this textbook was pro-Europe; we were daily fed this menu as part of our intellectual diets.

Many of my schoolmates, I am sure, can still remember vividly some of these nursery rhymes. They are:

- Percy the chick had a fall.
- Twisty and Twirly riding a bike to school.
- Pussycat, pussycat where have you been?
  I have been to London to visit the queen.
- Hey diddle, diddle, the cat and the fiddle,
  The cow jumped over the moon.

Most of my classmates did not have a book of their own (The West Indian Reader), so the teacher thought sharing was the logical thing to do. My teacher's name was Sincere Noel; she is the sister of my friend Annette Alexander, who later became a teacher herself. That afternoon, without alerting anyone, Sincere took our textbooks, divided the class into small groups, and appointed the person at the center as the one to hold the book while the rest of us took a peek and read along. Later that afternoon, I discussed this with my mother who jokingly said to me, "The next time they take your book, you tell them, "Dis nor fah-we, dis ah fo-meh." On hearing that, from my mother, I was bent on saying these words to any teacher who dared to take my book the way Sincere had. The following day my book was again taken. Instantly I opened my mouth and started to say, "Dis nor..." but I froze almost immediately and could not utter the remainder of that phrase. I realized that these words were foreign to my mouth and that I should have practiced saying them ahead of time. What the phrase dis nor fah-we, dis ah fo-meh means is "This doesn't belong to us; it belongs to me."

The above dialect is what was prevalent in Union Island years ago; it was what I had to assimilate quickly into, and I loved every bit of it. It was an intriguing journey indeed, one that was worth every minute of my time spent on that little rock.

Keep reading, folks, because "dis is weh ah we like, an, we na-e go no weh till we finish." (This is what we like, and we are not going anywhere until we are finished reading).

Things were happening quickly; we immediately became the owners of livestock. First we had a dog, then goats, sheep, pigs, fowl, and a cow, too. To my amazement, a few years later we would become the owners of the most goats in Union Island. We gave most of the goats our own names. These names were Lyris, Ezrard, Urias, Sheila, and so forth, and these animals responded to our call. Within a year, we were rearing most of these animals on one of the huge pastures of Ashton named Ms. Irene's Pasture. We were fond of the outdoors; we could go almost anywhere, and that meant freedom to us. My brother Urias and I woke up early each morning to look after our goats at that huge pasture. There we would meet with other chaps who also had their animals tied nearby.

Every Saturday, we would spend a tremendous amount of time at the pasture taking care of our animals. During those lengthy stays at this remote area, I had my first lesson on matters relating to the bathroom. When it was time to "go," we had to find a secluded area in the bush. There were literally no latrines available. I could also remember the times when we had no toilet tissue available, but we had to "go" nonetheless. As young chaps, we just had to improvise, using whatever was available. That could mean using the leaves of plants in the vicinity. It is easy to reminisce about my formative years and be flippant about it too, for those days rendered some intriguing experiences indeed. Many youngsters who reared livestock at those remote areas of the island will remember vividly and can relate to what I am talking about. Those days! Then as soon as we returned home from the pasture of Ms. Irene, we would be greeted with a glass of Aloe Vera juice mixed with milk. Our mother gave us that bitter drink once every month. God, how I hated it!

One Saturday afternoon while at the pasture of Ms. Irene, my dad took us farther into the dense vegetation of an area named Colon Campbell; there we found remnants of cotton plants from what is believed to be an old cotton plantation that once belonged to my great grand-father, John Henry Stewart. It was quite amazing to see the cotton plant for the first time. We were excited to lay our hands on the cotton and feel its texture. We placed a few of the partially opened cotton pods into our pockets, and then off we went again to look after our cow.

Back in Clifton, Ma and Grandma were doing fine, but Ma never ventured far from home; the most she did was walked slowly around the house with a wooden stick. Our visits to Clifton were mainly on Fridays, and we usually took Tiger Malts for her; it was her favorite beverage. We must have visited her at least nine times, and she always had something intriguing to say. She was a very humble woman who exhibited great affection toward us. One afternoon when we were about to say farewell to her, she asked, "Way all yo going now, Ashtin?" (She had meant Ashton). My mom nodded affirmatively, and off we went. It was the last time that I had seen her alive. I must admit that, during this short period, I had grown to love this old woman very much.

On the calm afternoon of January 22, 1969, exactly one year and five days after our arrival from Trinidad, this nonagenarian died peacefully at her home. She was only 96 years old. Her body was laid to rest on the following day at the Clifton Cemetery. She was gone. On that day, I saw my mother cry for the very first time.

My great-grandmother is gone, but she left with me some invaluable information, the details of which I will share in later chapters. I must admit that I was baffled for many years. Why did this old woman give to me such historical information that is more fitting for the mind of an adult? I questioned myself over and over again, but I guess she must have seen something in me.

Well, life at Campbell was very intriguing. During the 1970s at Basin Beach, I encountered many uncanny things that were very puzzling, and I was unable to decipher what was happening. I remained puzzled for many years; my callow mind did not permit me to comprehend what some of these incidents meant. Yet I remained mum and never shared with my peer what I had seen and heard. Later the memories did set off an unquenchable desire in me to write something that I could share with other Unionites such as myself and maybe the world.

When I was 18, the rest of my family had already returned to Trinidad, and I was bored to death living alone in the little house at Campbell. It was time for me to reunite with them, so on the calm afternoon of May 8, 1981; I left E.T. Joshua's Airport at Arnos Vale, St. Vincent, for Trinidad. I looked out of the plane just in time to take one last glimpse at the little wooden house until it disappeared before my eyes. After three hours, I was back in the district of Laventille, Trinidad, once again, having left it some 13 years earlier. A week later, my mom and I visited the Piccadilly Government School to see some of my former teachers. They were Ms. Harewood, Mrs. Farrell, and Mrs. Waite. Mrs. Farrell, my favorite teacher, had died only one month before we visited the school. Later that day I took my mother to a house where we had lived when I was only four years old, and then to the house that we had owned prior to leaving Trinidad for Union Island. She was startled at my phenomenal memory.

I was 19 years old now and wanted to write a book on Union Island, about things that were told to me, and also that which I had witnessed. Many facets of the island's history were unknown to us, and there was a lot to be learned. Our history studies at school were totally wrapped up in the history of Europe. Nothing of Africa or St. Vincent and the Grenadines was ever mentioned in our history books. We lauded the British Empire. Names such as Queen Elizabeth, Queen Isabella, King Ferdinand, John Hawkins, Walter Raleigh, Admiral Penn, General Venables, Francis Drake, and Henry Morgan were revered. Many of them were knighted "Sir" regardless of their notoriety. We were taught to respect and admire them nonetheless.

So I was bent on writing this book, and I had hastily accumulated forty-five pages on a notebook, which I kept with me at all times. My writing came to a gridlock a few months later. I didn't have the wherewithal to write a resourceful book that would do Union Island or me any good. My youthfulness and lack of experience were just added disadvantages. Coupled with that, I wrote almost the way I speak. At that time, my level of writing was way below the standard usage of grammar and mechanics that are required to write a resourceful book. This I attribute to my depressed experience during my formative years at Small School. The end came when I lost every piece of information that I'd saved.

The years were going by swiftly, with no notable events. Then suddenly I lost my grandmother Telina, the woman who had taken me from the harbor of Clifton to my great-grandmother at Point Lookout. She succumbed to a devastating stroke at her Point Lookout home. She fell in front of her doorstep and lay semiconscious for several hours. She was later taken to the Nurse Clouden Health Center at Clifton, were she was diagnosed and treated for hypertension. Unfortunately, she never regain consciousness and died a few days later. Her death was one of the most gruesome accidents that have ever happened on the island. Intracerebral hemorrhage was the culprit. On April 27, 1993, my grandmother Caroline (Telina) Roache was laid to rest beside her mother, Isabella, at the Clifton Cemetery. She was only 82 years old.

That was an extremely sad moment of my life, amid other challenges that I need not mention here; instead I will reference them in another book or maybe my autobiography in years to come.

Today I have made a concerted effort to start anew with my literary work by touching on every aspect of the lives of our people (Unionites). It is my hope that by doing so, I can document their authentic lifestyles in a manner that gives reverence to the ancestors—who they were and the impact they continue to have on us.

In remembrance of my great-grandmother, I erected a water well on Thursday, October 30th, 2013. This well, which is known as Well Isabella, is located at Point-look-Out where her house was situated. I could not think of anything else that represented life, longevity, and fulfillment of the life she had. It is at that setting that I was fed my first historical lesson. That location is where she evoked a penchant in me for the island's history; my mind's eye has been keenly opened since. Inadvertently, she changed my little world instantly and decisively. For many years after she died, I felt empty and alone. On many instances, it seemed as though my peers and me had little in common. I later saw myself as an anomaly.

Here I am today, and it's unbelievable how excited I am. I have so much to say that everything wants to seek an exit all at once, but I will take my time to touch on everything that my memory allows. These thoughts have saturated my mind for many years, almost my entire life. I will give my candid take on quite a few things that have slipped through the cracks; and perhaps offer a realistic peep into the not-too-distant future. Sounds a bit clairvoyant? Well, there are lots to talk about, so let's start with a slow, deliberate walk.

INTRODUCTION

Union Island Then and Now is a small but unique book that takes a comprehensive look at the lives and heritage of a people called "Unionites." It is my hope that the contents of this small manuscript that you are now holding firmly in your hands will be forever etched into your hearts and minds. You will know as never before, the island's history, heritage, and culture.

Now for all who once called Union Island home, this unique culture that is described here with honesty and candor will be relived by turning these crowded pages. Those who are not native to this region will automatically embrace the opportunity to learn and appreciate a new culture. This book's contents are intended to whet your appetites. Your reactions, I expect, will be contingent on how much you can identify with and relate to what is written. A word of caution! Some of the information here is unknown even to the few who once referred to Union Island as "Little England" during the mid-1970s.

This book speaks profoundly about evolution, something that no one can escape in his or her entire lifetime. However, for the purpose of simplicity, let us use the word change. Yet how many of us are happy with the change? "Change is the scariest word in the English language," author Dr. Susan Forward writes in her book, Emotional Blackmail. "No one likes it; almost everyone is terrified of it, and most people will become exquisitely creative to avoid it."

Unfortunately, many had failed miserably to accept things that differ from the way they were when they were growing up. Some changes are unavoidable, and some have significantly affected the social, economic, and academic growth of Union Island in a positive light. However, there is a need for watchdogs to sieve out other changes that may be regressive and counterproductive. This, of course, can engender productive growth.

For many years, Unionites in the Diaspora have watched from a distance the subtle transformations that have taken place from time to time. Although many of them abroad have taken the opportunity to make better their lives and in their settings, there is still a feeling of homesickness among them. That homesickness or nostalgia denotes a burning desire to return home someday, and of course "someday" means "permanently." Amid the myriad disadvantages in Union Island, some have returned permanently, releasing themselves from the gilded cages of the many countries abroad where they have been tethered for many years. Many others are still hopeful that they will be able to return someday and recapture some of the joys of their formative years. Well! This is not impossible, but they must be candidly informed or reminded that times have changed.

The following are the shared sentiments of many folks. They have articulated from their perspectives how time has changed in Union Island and the current mind-sets that correlate with those changes. Yet the yearning for the good old days still resurfaces continually. I suspect that many other Unionites may share some of the sentiments they expressed. These are some of their views:

"Look, I is ah big man eh, and ah know that time changing all the time. But it really hard to see the way things going on these days. Ah mean, when last you see them children nowadays play games like shick-shout, hopscotch, moral, green bush and marbles? This generation yah don't know nothing. You could tell them anything bout *both-head* when yo pitching marble? What about *Fenn-that, Go back to stars, Yo bringzing, Ah go suck them dry, or Yo getting bone-ox?* What is really going on today boy? Deh talking technology, advancement, modern time and ah whole set ah thing. But this technology-thing bringing more separation than anything else e-nor. Look at them cellphone them children have in da A's (ears). When them children standup close to you, and you calling them, you think dey does hear you? Eh...? Them children nah-e study you, and deh acting like they ain't dey dis side. Me ain't saying time can change and all that you know, no! That not what me saying, yo understand? What me is saying is, if you want technology, tek technology, is aright. Tek cellphone, tek computer. But for me? Help my Gad, give me long ago. I go settle wid that."

J.

"Growing up on Union Island was an experience that resulted in my conviction that I had the best childhood ever. Most of the customs and traditions are no more. Three things that I wished were still practiced in our culture are these:

Big Drum Dancing

The rhythm of the drums, the sensual movement of the women, and the demonstration of masculine control by the men are something to behold. The Douglas family had expertise in this area. It was a pleasure to watch them dance.

Sporting Events

Participants compete in traditional races such as Egg and spoon, Sack/bag race, One-leg race, Thread the needle, Rounders, Tug-a-war, and Maypole dancing. These games were fun to watch, and the entire family participated.

Moonlight Picnics

In the open pastures of Ashton, whether a church group, a community group, or just a few good friends spending time together, Moonlight never ended without fun, games, and food on some hillside on Union Island. Everyone contributed to the event, and one could hear singing and laughing from miles away. It was the sound of youthfulness and clean fun. Those days are gone!"

V.

"I can remember very well during the late 1960s and into the 1970s, when young men used to frequent the local beaches of Ashton to race some finely made sailing boats. Saturdays and Sundays were the days that they came out in numbers. Henry John and Ezzard Stewart had two of the finest sailing boats in Ashton. They were made from the local Pumpkin Wood tree, a lightweight wood that is easily moldable. I can tell you that these small yachts were splendidly made, and they sailed very well. Like the real thing, they had a spar, bowsprit, jib, mainsail, keel, and an adjustable rudder — the whole nine yards. And while this was a sport to be enjoyed, they had to be exceedingly careful not to take their eyes away from these small crafts while racing. Otherwise, they might easily lose their sailboats, for they could quickly sail away beyond their reach; they were really fast. This is something that is practiced no more in Union Island, not even the small Coconut boats that were flanked with a huge grape leaf and a tin rudder are available today. At least everyone could make those, even the girls. I would like to see those days re-surface."

K.

"You know what? I wish Union Island was still the same way it was when I was growing up. Those days was better days. People used to care more about each other -they had more unity, love, and togetherness! Today, em, you can see a lot of advancements, but with all of them new advancements, we have a lot of problems too. I don't like it you know. Drugs for one is too prevalent among the young people. Nobody wants to work, and they don't want to plant the land neither. Look nah! When I was growing up, everybody planted corn & peas, from Bottom Campbell in Ashton, all the way to Point look out, Clifton. Today, all you can see is bush. If you want ah roast-corn, way you getting it? "Stchups (sucks her teeth). People too selfish now. Give me ah break....You could put today with long ago? I for one rather the olden days."

Jenny.

So is the culture of Union island changing? The response here will be a resounding Yes! Thus far, it has changed significantly. Unionites are experiencing their culture steadily dwindling its way into permanent oblivion, and the question that perplexes most is this: Should they be blamed for looking back constantly as Lot's wife did in biblical history? Older folks will agree that even the important folktales such as Bra. Ananci and the redoubtable fibs or fiction of the La Diablesse stories listened to during their formative years are solely held in their tenuous palms, figuratively speaking. Unfortunately, these folktales may expire with them unless there is some redoubtable force that is resilient to this downward spiral of the culture in Union Island.

The story about Bra Anansi Spider is a folk tale from the tradition of the Ashanti people of Ghana, Africa. Bra Anansi (imaginary figure) was very cunning, as always; he played tricks on other animals to get them to do what he wanted. The La

Diablesse story is yet another folktale that places fear in the heart and minds of listeners. La Diablesse is nocturnal and is perceived to be a female with fine appearance who lures her victims (men) away from home into dark wooded areas. The victim is lost, and stumbles to find his way back home. The feet of the La Diablesse sometimes change into a hoof like that of a cow. A memorable incident is when some Diablesse were taken to Frigate Rock via a rowboat; they paid the fishermen two shilling and five pence and then leaped off the boat just before it arrive at Frigate Rock, ran onto the little island, then shouted, "Look in your hands—goat shit, goat shit." The Soucouyant, like the La Diablesse, is another sinister character that travels at night—is said to possess the power of flight.

Inevitably, the above folktales and many more will expire within another decade or so unless this current heedless spiral comes to an abrupt end. Some may say, "Well old ideas have been supplanted by new ideas," which is an eventual state of acceptance. The truth is, extinction is gradually making its presence felt while many hopelessly looked on. "Long time, long ago, or back when," are already some of the choice words that have become an active part of our vocabularies whenever Union Island is mentioned. Many will agree.

The long and hopefully enjoyable presentation of education and cultural reminders that are etched within the binding of this book will begin immediately in the chapters that follow. This book possesses some essential information and references for many, and may serve as an instrument of strength or fortitude. From a morbid yet realistic point of view, one can only surmise that the end is wrapped up in the brevity of time. In the meantime, Unionites must salvage and savor as fine jewelry what is left of that rich culture because it appears that those footprints in the sand of time are fading quickly into utter oblivion...

Now, sit back, relax, and enjoy this meager but significant reminder of Union Island's history in Union Island Then and Now.

Easily accessible hotels, guesthouses, and inns at Clifton Harbor

♦♦♦□*Chapter One*

WHERE IS UNION ISLAND?

The Impetus to write UITN, that precedes this subject, states that Union Island is situated some 180 miles north of Trinidad. Without a shadow of doubt, this island is relatively unknown to the outside world. Nevertheless, this island is safely situated in the heart of the Caribbean. With the advent of the personal computer, sites such as Google Earth have given justice to our shores by providing ubiquitous access to just about every place known. To access this member of the archipelago on Google Earth and to have a panoramic view of her neighboring sister islands, one can search 12 degrees, 35', 48.96" North and 61 degrees, 25', 49.43" West.

You may wonder about the source of the island's name. Surely it came from Mr. Samuel A. Spann, a slave trader whose history you are about to read. Samuel co-owned a ship during the 1850s that bore the name Union Island, so it is safe to deduce that he named the island after his ship. Ashton and Clifton, the two small villages of Union Island, were also names that originated from suburbs in Great Britain. During the 19 Century up until the 1950s, Clifton, the capital, was widely referred to as *Calsay*, while Ashton, the western part of the island, was called *Frigate* because of its affinity to Frigate Island (rock).

Union Island is one of the larger islands of the Southern Grenadines. The Grenadines, in turn, are a chain of very small islands between two major islands of the Windward Islands in the West Indies. These two major islands are Grenada and St. Vincent. St. Vincent is situated more to the north while its sister, Grenada is in the south. St. Vincent governs most of these small islands. Proximity might be the deciding factor here. Petit

Martinique and Carriacou, on the other hand, are two other small Islands of the south that are governed by Grenada. Unfortunately for Union Island, during the 1890s and the early 20th Century, the sentiments of the residents were sometimes mixed as to which of these major islands (St. Vincent and Grenada) should assume ownership. A detailed look at this situation will be taken in another chapter.

Grenada, often referred to as "the island of spice," became known worldwide during the 1980s when its prime minister, Maurice Bishop, was assassinated, and the American Armed Forces later rescued the island from rebels.

The second largest and next to the most southerly of the Grenadine Islands of St. Vincent, Union Island was deemed the artistic center and cultural Mecca of the Grenadines for many years.

To any visitor who has visited St. Vincent but has not yet laid foot on the birthplace of our luminary, the honorable Captain Hugh Mulzac, you must be reminded that you have not yet honored your right to exploration and discovery. Hugh Mulzac? Yes, this is a household name that everyone will become more familiar with after reading this book.

Though it is common knowledge that the redoubtable TV personality Oprah Winfrey once sailed on a convoy of yachts to the island of Mustique, she, too, is not absolved from the responsibility of laying her feet on the precious soil of Union Island. It is reputed that she may have been in the waters of Palm Island and Petit St. Vincent—a stone's throw away from Union Island. This, however, may still be good news for the region in that her return to these white sandy shores is surely imminent.

The Union Island that many have grown to love over the years is virtually unknown to the world. The world, as many may look at it, is only as wide and as vast as their minds are programmed and conditioned to see it. So, in fact, many may not see the world exactly as it is in most cases but only as their paradigms allow. Keep in mind that for 99 percent of the world out there, there is no such place as Union Island. Though still referred to as the "Little Tahiti of the West Indies" by an infinitesimal few, very little is known of this minuscule landmass.

If anyone were to walk the well-trodden streets of Manhattan in New York, from 42nd Street Times Square to Malcolm X Boulevard, 125th Street, with a large map bearing the words "Union Island," and if ten or more people were to identify with that island, then it can be said a monumental task have been accomplished. But there is great doubt that this will ever happen. So the task of writing this book encompasses the responsibility of conveying to the larger world the presence of the Grenadines of St. Vincent as a significant entity. But for now, Union Island is the primal focus.

Union Island now possesses a small but racially integrated community, and this may be a plus to engender growth from several aspects of the business environment. Therefore, it is imperative that information be disseminated to the outside world of the African influences, mores, folkways, conventions, and local customs that are still pervasive in this unfamiliar territory.

UNION ISLAND VISITED

Spanning the shores of Point Lookout, the beautiful beaches of Basin, Campbell, Richmond, Big-Sand, Belmont, Bloody Bay, Rapid, and of course, the exclusivity of Chatham Beach in the Western side of the island, will all give an insurmountable feeling of blithe. There is energy, a combined collective force working in concert here. There is synergy, a union. And so the name Union Island is quite appropriate to meet all of its intangibles.

The beaches and rocky terrain are nothing short of breeding grounds for tourists who came in droves, eager to enjoy the unadulterated beauty that God and Nature have created. They immediately become cognizant of the sheer liberty that exists in this beautiful southern part of Grenadines Island. Experience will later teach that such levels of joyous nonchalance can only be exhibited in these tropical virgin territories such as Union Island and a host of neighboring cays. Although not big on nightlife, the accommodating staffs at Anchorage Hotel, Bouginvilla Hotel, Kings Landing Hotel, Clifton Beach Hotel, Big-Sand Hotel, Islander's Inn Hotel, Palm Island Resort & Spa, and Lambi's Guest House are unquestionably second to none when it comes to hospitality. Mustique Island, an excellent neighboring resort island, is also a little gem that is known around the entire globe. Yes! This is exactly where Union Island is situated. Like Union Island, these 31 other neighboring islands are gracefully flanked by the ubiquitous trade winds of the Atlantic Ocean.

It seems almost unbelievable that Union Island has been inhabited since 5400 BC. With that said, it is unrealistic to believe that the world is 2000 years old as once taught by the churches in the Caribbean. It is equally unrealistic to give credit to what history has taught us about Christopher Columbus. His presence in the Caribbean or so-called New World in the year 1492 may have given rise to a newfound knowledge in Europe, and Europe only. It is not by accident the 'The Burning Spear, a Jamaican reggae artist, refers Christopher Columbus as a "damn blasted liar, "indicating that the islands of the Caribbean were already

4

inhabited long before his so-called discovery of the New World. Mutabaruka, another singer/poet from Jamaica referred to him as "Christopher-Come-Bust-Us" for the taints that are attached to his name.

It is clear that Christopher Columbus had visited the Caribbean some 6892 or more years after this little rock had already been inhabited. But what was it called by the first inhabitants? That we will never Know. On January 22, 1498, Christopher Columbus (Spanish) landed on St. Vincent, but no information is available to substantiate that he actually laid foot on this little rock now called Union Island. During the presence of the Spanish in the region, they observed the Grenadines as a group of tiny islands closely aligned like a flock of birds. They named these islands Los Pajoros which means the birds.

When Christopher Columbus arrived in the region, the Amerindian tribes of South America were right here on Union Island. Archeological studies have confirmed their presence from 5400 BC up until the 1760s. The Amerindians were the Carib tribe whose origin lies in the southern West Indies and the northern coast of South America. Today, in Union Island there is no documented history or trace of the descendants of this once noble tribe since the French inhabited the island in the 1760's. It is paramount that their disappearance be questioned and researched in hopes of amending the island's history and her-story.

The numerous artifacts found on the soil of Union Island provide further proof of the existence of this tribe up until the 1760s. During the 1970s and beyond, many of these artifacts were unearthed from where they were hidden, including beneath the many Manchineel trees that are found on every beach on the island. Foreign archeologists have visited and studied this pristine territory as well as the lives and customs of the Amerindians. They finally made good of the spoils, which they unearthed without consent from local authorities. It is reputed that all ancient cutlery, potsherds, vessels, bowls, and cylinders have been removed from Union Island by those archeologists. It is further reputed that some of these artifacts have been sold at exorbitant prices at foreign museums in the Americas while others remained as exhibits at various museums as well. Currently, there are no museums available on Union Island that reflect the presence of this once noble tribe, their lives, or the rich tangible legacy they unwittingly left behind.

The Manchineel plant mentioned above is considered one of the most poisonous tree species in the world. The Spanish called the fruits of the Manchineel tree "little apples of death."The milk or sap of this plant is a potent skin irritant. Even standing under this plant during a heated day was widely discouraged because doing so would cause severe skin blisters. Eating the fruit is fatal. The Amerindians (Caribs and Arawaks) used the milky sap of this plant to poison their arrows during hunting and also against their enemies. It was also reputed that the leaves were sometimes used to poison the water of their enemies. The numerous Manchineel trees that were present at Chatham Bay, coupled with the unearthed artifacts at that site, have substantiated the presence of these first natives.

Now, it must be remembered that it was the appearance of the French in the neighboring island of Grenada during the 1650s that led to a bloody battle with the Amerindians (Carib) residents. In the 1650s, a French expedition from the Caribbean island of Martinique landed on Grenada and established a so-called friendly rapport with the natives. Hostility became inevitable as the French exhibited their desire to control the entire island. War broke out almost immediately between the two factions when the Amerindians demonstrated unwillingness to submit to these settlers.

The Amerindians put up fierce resistance in a succession of battles but were eventually defeated. Rather than surrender to their soon-to-be successors, the remaining tribe members chose the hills of Sauteurs, North Grenada, where they committed suicide by leaping off a cliff to their eventual deaths. The French later named the spot "Le Morne de Sauteurs," or "Leapers' Hill. The question must now be asked: Did the Amerindians of Union Island just give up the island to these foreign settlers/invaders, or did they put up fierce resistance, which would have been true to their nature? Whatever happened, these communal people were never seen again on this island after the French settled during the 1760s. Unfortunately, the history (and her-story) of the indigenous people of Union Island was never documented, or made available for history books.

In the late 1750s, Antoine Regaud and Jean Augier, two French merchants from Martinique and Guadeloupe set foot on

Union island. It was during this time that this archipelago of islands was named the Grenadines. These two Frenchmen were deemed the principal settlers of the island. Were the Amerindians gone by this time? Certainly not! Today, many people are still eager to find out how the northernmost bay of Union Island (Bloody Bay) got its name. The activities that took place at this bay may be synonymous with those of the renowned Le Morne De Sauteurs (Leapers Hill) of Grenada.

These Frenchmen were deeply entrenched in the lucrative slave trade. They brought with them 350 slaves and initiated the commercial planting of cotton, a plant that remained visible in the dense bushes of Colon Campbell until the 1970s. The historical foundation of Union Island began with the presence of a very wealthy merchant of Bristol, England, named Samuel Spann during the mid 1760s. This wealthy British merchant was heavily involved in slave trade and general maritime trade under the banner of S & J Spann and Company (Samuel and John, his brother). It is reputed that S & A was also involved in piracy, and as a result, they lost several of their ships. Like the Frenchmen, Samuel and his brother John bought hundreds of slaves from Cameroon, Angola, and other ports of Africa. It is reputed that a third brother (Spann), whose first name is unknown had been on the island for some time. He later left to pursue business in Trinidad, one of the larger islands of the Caribbean.

In 1778, the population of Union Island had increased quite a bit. There were now sixteen Europeans (ten French and six English), with a workforce exceeding 400 slaves and a bountiful cotton crop that collectively yielded a substantial harvest annually. Two hundred and fifty thousand (£250,000) British pounds per year was surely rewarding. The British and French coexisted on the little island for more than a decade. But with the Treaty of Paris on February 10, 1763, the British were ushered in as the rulers of the region. This substantiated the fact that two forces cannot occupy the same space at the same time. Subsequently, Samuel Spann, the British merchant, assumed ownership of the island. Regaud, one of the two French settlers, disappeared immediately. Augier, on the other hand, remained on the island for a number of years but finally left.

Mr. Spann, whose principal home was in Bristol, England, subsequently made Union Island his entrepreneurial home. Other Members of the Spann family also descended on Union Island to enjoy the fruits of early industry and economy. They inevitably became the principal residents on the island as the family grew in numbers. They buried their loved ones at their private burial Ground at Gardenfield, Ashton, as opposed to the older cemetery that is located in the vicinity of Petit Bay at Clifton Harbor. The Spann's burial ground was fenced, but among the tombs were numerous orange and plum trees. Visiting this old site, one can still see the boundary of the once fenced plot of land. Pictures of a few badly eroded tombstones can be seen on the following website www.unionislandbooks.com. Two tombstones are partially intact in that old cemetery. They are engraved with the names Mariana Spann, who was the wife of Oliver Spann, and Lavinia Cuthbert, the first wife of Richard P. Mulzac, (mentioned later) and the mother of his first two sons, John and Edward.

The legacy of cotton farming continued under the S & J banner for almost one hundred years. With the abolition of slavery fifty-one years later in the West Indies (1834) came a change of tide on the plantation. The lucrative cotton industry never returned to its former stature. Sixteen years later, in 1850, S & J Spann and Company had seen enough to call it a day. That same year the company sold the island to Major Collins, a resident of St. Vincent.

With little to do on the island in terms of generating an easy income, many of the Spann family went back to England in pursuit of better life. It is reputed that some migrated to the United States while others went to the nearby island of Trinidad, where another faction of the Spann family resided.

Integration has always been akin to slavery; so many of the Spann families of Union Island were also mixed with slaves and other blacks that arrived from Antigua and Barbados. They were the majority (Spann) to remain on Union Island post-slavery, resulting in an expansion of the bloodline. Today, although traces of the Spann bloodline are still evident on the island, the Spann family name has dwindled to an alarming zero. This may be due in part to the fact that many young women (Spann) who married may have been compelled to assume the family names of their husband. Nonetheless, the principal contributing factor must be attributed to the legacy of migration, a system that will be explained in detail in another chapter. In humility, the author referred to it as The Exodus Factor. It has become an integral part of the life and legacy of every Unionite, and by extension, anyone who have lived in Union Island for a considerable amount of years. Unfortunately!

CHARLES MULZAC'S LEGACY

In 1863, a Scottish sharecropper took an interest in Union Island and later leased it from Major Collins for £150 per year. That Scottish sharecropper was Mr. Charles Mulzac. Charles' influence on this little island was profound; it further shaped, molded and fashioned the island's culture, an impact that is still evident today after 150 years. He was the grandfather of Hugh Mulzac, now a household name in St. Vincent and the Grenadines.

Charles came to Union Island with his wife and four children: Richard, Mary, Emma, and John. At such time, Richard, his oldest son, was only twelve years old. Unlike the Spann family, whose interest was limited to cotton, the Mulzac family became dominant entrepreneurs throughout the island. Celebrated for their enormous skill in shipbuilding, the young men of this family manned many cargo vessels throughout the region. They were also adept at whaling and fishing, which they did extensively in the islands of Grenadines. With the cotton crop forcefully kept alive, Union Island was also rife with livestock, and the Mulzacs were the sole supplier of the island's milk and meats.

It is over 150 years since Charles Mulzac laid foot on Union Island, yet many first names of the early Mulzac family are still evident in the younger generations. Names such as Charles, Ada, Una, Roselyn, Hugh, Richard, and Edward can still be found in the family as descendants take honor and pride in bearing these names with dignity.

Richard Mulzac, Charles' first son, married his sweetheart, Lavina Cutbert (white woman), while he was still a teenager; she was three years his senior. She bore him two sons, John and Edward. Unfortunately, Lavina became extremely ill and later died on January 28, 1878; she was only 28 years old. She was buried at the Spann's cemetery at Gardenfield. In 1885, seven years after Lavina's death, Richard wedded Ada Donowa, a woman of African descent whose parents were from Antigua, in the Leeward Islands. From this marital union began the life and legacy of a legendary hero and a historic giant named Hugh Mulzac. Richard and Ada had seven children: Hugh, Irvin, Una, Lavina, Lamie, James, and May. Richard affectionately named one of his daughters Lavina, the name of his deceased wife.

The tomb of Lavinia Cuthbert, Richard Mulzac's first wife.

Fully aware that the institution of slavery was no more, or at least had dwindled in its physical abuse of the Africans, Hugh's grandfather, Charles, elected to use sharecropping in a stringent manner to keep the cotton industry afloat. This method had a tragic, long-lasting impact on farmers (Africans) of Union Island.

Sharecropping was a system of agriculture in which a landowner allowed a tenant to use the land in return for a share of the crops that he or she produced on that land (e.g., 50 percent of the crop). Unfortunately, there was no significant economic change; sharecropping did little to boost the local economy. It is reputed that Charles Mulzac elected to receive 66 percent as his allotment of the crops. He bought from the Africans their 33 percent allotment of the cotton crop, but paid so little that it was utterly senseless for them to remain farmers on the plantations. With little to attain through their tedious efforts on those plantations, the Africans developed an aversion to working the land. This aversion has spiraled down through generations and is notably evident today.

As a result, conditions on the plantations were deplorable,

and many blacks refused to work hard. This recalcitrant attitude of blacks on the plantation escalated when Mr. E. Richards, a merchant from St. Vincent, assumed ownership of Union Island during the threshold of the 20th Century. The distressful condition on the plantation was way over a decade old. It was during that time that Isabella Roache, made mentioned of. A sick black man who begged for his life to be spared, "Massa me nah dead yet, Massa me nah dead yet." Unfortunately, his cry fell on obstinate ears, for he was later buried alive. "Carry um go bury um," (take him and bury him) was the last order given by the plantation owner to have his subject buried alive. Why was this still happening on the plantation? The answer is simple. It is because the "Massa-slave" relationship was still existent on the plantation long after the abolition of slavery in 1834. As a result, the so-called "free" slaves were still dependent on their superiors as the patriarchs of the island.

The yield of the cotton crop continued to decline significantly. Several years before Charles Mulzac's death in 1893, his first son, Richard, assumed command of all his assets and businesses. The 66 percent allotment Charles had claimed for sharecropping was not an asset to the steadily declining economy of that day. Furthermore, the 33 percent of the spoils that Africans received from selling their cotton to Richard Mulzac was worth next to nothing. Hardship was strongly felt by these Africans who continued to be troubled by the uncertainty of the cotton crop, their only source of income. They shifted their focus heavily to cultivating other crops such as cassava, potatoes, fruits, corn, and pigeon peas, which they also had to share with Charles, and later Richard.

The latter two crops flourished bountifully each year and quickly became the main crops of the island. Yet life remained a challenge for those farmers because these two crops did not generate an income. Life remained difficult, and the aversion to working the land escalated drastically. For they wanted to do better, but there was nowhere to turn. It prompted many young chaps and fathers to leave the island in search of greener pastures. Leaving wasn't that easy, for they first had to have somewhere to go. Some young men never left at all, and unfortunately, most who did never returned

The reality is that there was nothing attainable financially on those plantations other than the food, which they were able to consume themselves. Could they abandon agriculture? No! For there was nowhere these people could have turned. Unfortunately, this tacit aversion to working the land had been handed down throughout the years and has placed today's generation at a deficit on the farmlands. Hence it is not a surprise that the corn and pea crops of Union Island are eventually at it's lowest.

With the state of the declining economy, the Windward Island hurricane of September 1898 further devastated the cotton industry of Union Island. Miraculously, the tenuous cotton crop was still alive on many farms, but at that time it was insignificant low compared to its original stature.

Having experienced all these major challenges, Richard Mulzac, the father of nine children unwittingly surrendered the land ownership back to Major Collins at the turn of the twentieth Century. This was exactly seven years after his father's death in 1893. It was the end of a lease that had continued for almost five decades.

Richard remained the go-to person where cotton was concerned. He processed the raw cotton with the sole cotton gin on the island. With the help of his sons Irvin, John and Edwards, Richard focused his attention on shipbuilding and making a living at sea. Richard and his family were some of the principal owners of vessels in the region. As in the neighboring island of Bequia, whaling was an art that was also practiced in Union Island, and the Mulzac boys were no slouch. Whales were butchered on Frigate Island (Rock). John, his first son, was a fierce captain at sea. He manned the Sunbeam (ship) throughout the Caribbean waters for several years. He later fell victim to the unpredictable regional waters during a hurricane in 1921. At that time, he was bringing his vessel, the Evelyn Guy, into port. Since then, countless lives of local seamen have been lost at sea; a subject that will be discussed in a subsequent chapter.

After Richard Mulzac relinquished the lease of Union Island to an aged Major Collins, the island was immediately sold in 1901-2 to Mr. E. Richards, a merchant of St. Vincent. Mr. E. Richards was the grandfather of Van, Lincoln, and Emerita Richards, now residing in the USA, Margaret of Tobago, and the late Dick Richards (mentioned later). Mr. Richards' rulership represented one of the worst life's experiences for the people of

Union Island. With the already depressed economic crises, pestering the land, health and living conditions continued to deteriorate drastically under Mr. E. Richard's oppressive rulership. Yet the landlord took no salutary action to amend the plight of the ailing land. But by that time, these Africans who had nothing to call their own, had seen enough, and hence refused to be pliable to this tyrant. At best, he was making life a hell for them. On the brink of rebellion, they forcefully presented a petition to the administrator of that day on September 30th, 1909, requesting that the Government assume immediate ownership of the island, the establishment of a peasant proprietary, and an annexation to Grenada. Unfortunately, Grenada could not shoulder such financial responsibility and Union Island remained under the ordinance of St. Vincent.

With so many injustices on the land, Mr. E. Richards was pressured into selling it to the British Government or Crown on June 1, 1910 for £5,000. At that point, it was referred to as "Crown Lands. "The British Crown then subdivided the land into parcels of two, three, and four acres. The residents were able to buy lands; they felt a sense of ownership by truly owning something of value for the first time. As a result, they felt liberated. The first sale began in 1911, immediately after the Crown assumed possession. So deeds granted to landowners during those early years would bear the following caption:

Saint Vincent.

GEORGE V. by the Grace of God of Great Britain, Ireland and of the British Dominions beyond the Seas King, Defender of the Faith Emperor of India.

To all of whom these presents shall come.

Know Ye that in consideration of the sum of *three* Pound.................shilling and...........Pence paid by *Charles Stewart* of *Union Island*...........................to the treasurer of our said Colony of St. Vincent we do hereby grant unto the said *Charles Stewart* and his heirs all that piece or portion of land situated on the acquired Estate of *Union Island* in the parish of *Southern Grenadines* in the said colony of St. Vincent being one *lot* in the extent number *19* and bounded as shown and described in the diagram heron and also on the plan recorded in the office of the superintendent of works or however otherwise the same may be bounded known or described. Together with all buildings and appurtenance and easements thereto belonging. To have and to hold the said piece or portion of land to the said *Charles Stewart* his heirs and assigns for ever subject however to any Regulations made by the "Governor in Council" under the provision of "The Land Settlement Ordinance 1899" and the conditions therein continued. If the said *Charles Stewart* shall fail to comply with the said Regulations, the Present grant may, pursuant to the said Regulation of any time after such failure be revoked by US or the Officer Administrating the Government of our said Colony of St. Vincent and the said piece or portion of land may be dealt with pursuant to the said Regulations.

The Crown reserves to itself the fee simple out of the grant hereby made all mines, veins, beds, deposits or accumulation of Minerals and Mineral Oil already found; or which may hereafter be found under the premises aforesaid with full liberty at all times for the Crown to enter and inspect the same, for the purpose searching for, getting, winning and taking away the said Mineral and Mineral Oil, subject to such compensation for injury done to or upon the surface, or any building standing thereon as may be determined by two arbitrators of whom one shall be appointed on behalf of the Crown and the other by and on behalf of the Grantee, or such other private party (if any) interested for the time being in the said premises, or in the event of disagreement between such arbitrators, such compensation as may be determined by an umpire, who shall be appointed in writing by such arbitrators before they enter on the matter so referred to them or on any matter upon which such arbitrators may differ, and in such event the decision of the umpire thereon shall be final and binding.

In testimony whereof we have caused these Our Letters

to be made Patent and the Great Seal of Our said Colony to be hereto affixed. *Witness our trust and well beloved James henry garret esquire,* office administration and Government of Our said Colony of St. Vincent this *23rd* day of *September 1911* and in the *twenty-first* Year of Our Reign.

WilliamP. Dolly F. S. 1
Superintendent of works

Date of allotment.
11:11:1911.

It is evident that the above document is a true exhibition of the Old English. This Old English is still used in the legal system of St. Vincent & the Grenadines and is very difficult for the layman to understand.

Now, with Africans being landowners of the same land that they once worked for their superiors, they were able to reap the entire benefits of their labor. Unfortunately, the price of the cotton remained very low. The Mulzacs, on the other hand, who were the sole buyers, were not willing to give the farmers more for their produce. As a result, many young men were now forced to pursue work in new frontiers to take care of their families. Some left Union Island on boats such as the Sunbeam, Lady Osprey, Ocean King, and Wanderer, which conducted trade in the region. Others ventured to Europe and America in hopes of improving their standard of living. Unfortunately, many were never seen in the region again.

With boatbuilding being introduced to the island by the Mulzac family, some young men had the opportunity to learn the skill of shipwright. With that remarkable skill, the gloomy future of the island seemed to be disappearing quickly. A few years later, many youngsters became owners of several small fishing boats and vessels, which they built themselves. The lumber to build these crafts was obtained from the forest of Colon Campbell.

During those years, Colon Campbell was rife with cedar trees that were planted during the years when the French and

English inhabited the island. During the 1930s up until the 1970s, many Unionites had owned vessels, and they conducted interisland trade throughout the Caribbean. With this type of business venture, the economy of Union Island was in better standing than during the tumultuous years of sharecropping. The names of several vessels that were owned by Unionites are listed in another chapter.

During the first quarter of the 20th century, many of the Mulzac families left Union Island and ventured abroad for greener pastures. Traces of this family are present in the USA. They are primarily the descendants of Hugh and his younger brother James. During such time, the Mulzac's entrepreneurial power in Union Island began to dwindle. Two remarkable residents came to prominence almost immediately. They were Joseph Alves (Daddy Alves) and Allan Scrubb (Ba Allan). As vessel owners, they conducted marine trade in the region and were successful entrepreneurs.

Daddy Alves, born in the neighboring island of Carriacou during the 1870's, was also a shopkeeper of Union Island from the 20's to the 50's. He was fond of Union Island and hence made the village of Ashton his home. His wife, Edith, who was born in the neighboring island of Bequia in 1885, was the teenage girlfriend of Hugh Mulzac before he left in 1907 for his endeavors at sea. Daddy Alves and his wife Edith was loved and respected by Unionites. This Kayak (native of Carriacou) with his thick accent, was noted for a line he coined some seventy-plus years ago: *Vincentians, from collar & tie to barefoot, none nar good.* This translates to Vincentians from the highest echelons of society to those in the throes of poverty are considered to be untrustworthy. This saying is still recited by a few older folks whenever Daddy Alves' name is mentioned. Allan Scrubb (Ba Allan), another entrepreneur in his own right, was also a fine shopkeeper at Ashton village. He was the first resident to build a concrete house on the island. He completed this task in the year 1922.

Today, though Unionites seldom own vessels like those of yesterday, they are proud owners of very small fishing boats that can easily comb the waters of the Grenadines. Of the legacy left from Richard Mulzac, the entrepreneurial mastermind of Union Island, boatbuilding and whaling are completely extinct. Although Interisland marine trade has diminished considerably over the years, animal husbandry, and fishing remains an active part of the island's culture.

HUGH NATHANIEL MULZAC

The Honorable Captain Hugh Nathaniel Mulzac was born on March 26, 1886, in Ashton Village. Like his father and two older brothers, John and Edward, young Hugh had a natural disposition for sea life. As a boy on Union Island, during his first time out in a rowboat, he lost control during a heavy current and had to be rescued by his father's friends. Hugh indicated that he got the beating of a lifetime from his father. On March 12, 1907, Hugh left the shores of Union Island to improve his fortune, as he stated later in his autobiography. It was the last time that he saw his father and other close members of his family. On February 14, 1930, his father Richard P. Mulzac died and was buried at the Ashton Cemetery by Hugh's younger brother Irvin Mulzac. Richard was 79 years old.

Captain Hugh Mulzac in his latter years

Yes, Hugh's remarkable marine life of courage and fortitude began immediately after his tenure at high school at St. Vincent. After a brief sailing experience on the Sunbeam, a 90-ton schooner engaged in island trade and manned by his older brother John, Hugh bid the region farewell. In March 1907, he left the harbor of Bridgetown, Barbados, on a ship named the Aeolus (A Star to Steer by). A tall blond Norwegian named Granderson was the captain. They sailed first to North Carolina, America, then to Europe. After several voyages with the Aeolus, he bid Captain Granderson farewell to pursue better opportunities. He later served on several British schooners as an efficient seaman, but later returned to America.

Hugh later became a resident of America and resided in the state of Maryland. In 1916 he married a pretty woman by the name of Sadie Moore. That year, they had one daughter whose name was Elaine. Regrettably his marriage ended in divorce a few years later. In 1918, two important things happened for Hugh. On December 9, 1918 he became a US citizen, then two weeks later he sat for his shipmaster's license and passed it. This license qualified him to command a ship, but he was never given the opportunity to do so because racism was still the order of the day. Two years later on September 30, 1920. Hugh Mulzac married Marie Avis, a native of Jamaica; they would have four children. They were Joyce, Una, Claire and Hugh Jr.

In 1942, during World War II, he became the first African-American to command a ship in the United States Merchant Marine. The name of the ship was the SS Booker T. Washington. This was an assignment met with great disapproval by the establishment prior to him being considered for such a task. Although he had been qualified for some twenty-four years yet was denied such an opportunity, his perseverance and propensity for such a herculean task had never waned.

With a crew of eighteen nationalities under his captaincy, he manned the SS Booker T. Washington through the seas of Europe and the Pacific. There he made twenty-two round trips over a period of five years and had a troop of approximately 18,000. In his book A Star to Steer By, he deemed one of the happiest days of his life the day he walked onto the Booker T. Washington's bridge. He stated, "There really are no words to express how I felt that evening when the final 'I' was dotted, and final 't' crossed, and I was master of my own vessel. "Everything

I ever was, stood for, fought for, dreamed of, came into focus that day. The concrete evidence of the achievement gives one's strivings legitimacy, proves that the ambitions were valid, the struggle worthwhile. Being prevented for those twenty-four years from doing the work for which I was trained had robbed life of its most essential meaning. Now at last I could use my training and capabilities fully. It was like being born anew."

Today, the name Hugh Mulzac is a household name in St. Vincent and the Grenadines. His achievement is a symbol of pride and strength to the people. He is an inspiration to every Vincentian at home and abroad. The bitter truth is that the Honorable Captain Hugh Mulzac's life was a testimony of hard work, struggle, and disenfranchisement from the day he left the Caribbean Sea for a better life north of the equator.

Being the son of the principal entrepreneur on Union Island, young Hugh Mulzac had a privileged upbringing. His Grandfather Charles and father were Caucasians from Scotland; hence, young Hugh was considered "near white" by most residents in the Caribbean—a negative impact of slavery, which enabled the descendants of slaves to look at the high melanin content of their own skins as negative. Hugh's numerous encounters of racial prejudice have been particularly daunting compared to the good life he left behind on Union Island. Undeterred, the young chap persevered.

Another young man Hugh's age was Bine Stewart. He also left Union Island during the years 1906-1907. This young lad, who had been a sailor for several years, found life easier in America, where he worked very hard and sent his money back home to his father John. Like Captain Hugh Mulzac, he was not absolved from the wrath of racism. For although slavery had been abolished on paper, we full well know otherwise. Several years after he obtained a job in America, he succumbed to an untimely death provoked by racism. This strong black stallion was brutally hanged in the city of New Orleans, Louisiana. Unfortunately, the dead remains of Mr. Bine were never returned to his family in Union Island for proper burial.

Hugh's exodus from Union Island during his early years established a migratory trend that has since become a legacy; one that may never meet its demise among today's generations. Nevertheless, Hugh's life at sea was typical of the numerous fathers of Union Island who left their wives back at home to sail on the National Bulk ships just to make ends meet. They returned home once every year, but then only for a short period of time. Then off again to their lives at sea, leaving their wives pregnant one more time. Nevertheless, Hugh's achievement abroad earned him much respect from the natives of St. Vincent and the Grenadines and from the world as well. To honor Hugh Mulzac for his historical contribution in the global black community, the Captain Hugh Mulzac Square was created at Clifton Harbor, Union Island, at the turn of the 21 Century.

During the 1960s, Captain Hugh returned to the land of his birth for the only time since his departure in March of 1907; it was the last time he would see the island he once called home.

On January 31, 1971, at the ripe old age of 84, Captain Hugh Nathaniel Mulzac died and was buried at East Meadow in Long Island, New York. Unfortunately, at the time of his death, he was not recognized for the contribution he made as a serviceman. Surviving him at such time were his son Hugh Mulzac Jr. and his four daughters, Mrs. Elaine Hackley, Mrs. Joyce Chamberlayne, Una Mulzac, and Clair Mulzac. May his rest be long and peaceful.

The burial site of Hugh Nathaniel Mulzac in Queens, New York. A grave that is situated thousands of miles from the little village of Ashton, Union Island where he was born.

THE EXODUS FACTOR

During the time of the Spann's entrepreneurial presence in Union Island (1760's-1850's), they did fairly well with the lucrative cotton industry, but they left soon after the industry took a nosedive upon encountering financial impediments. The two French merchants, Antoine Regaud and Jean Augier, left the island several decades before the Spanns, for they were negatively affected by the Treaty of Paris of February 10, 1763.

In 1863 when Charles Mulzac leased Union Island from Major Collins of St. Vincent, he brought with him his four young children. It appeared that he came to the region to settle. He did. He governed the island for three decades, and with his method of governance, his eldest son Richard later became the entrepreneurial mastermind on the island. They amassed hundreds of livestock and supplied milk and meat for the entire island. They were excellent fishermen, whalers, and boat builders, and they conducted inter-island marine trade in the region. They also monopolized the cotton industry; hence they were the only ones who made a profit from it. In essence, the Mulzac family was financially sound.

On March 12, 1907, the island's prodigy, Hugh Mulzac who was just turning twenty, left Union Island to pursue his navigational career and life at sea. Later that year, he ended up in America. During such time, he maintained his burning desire to return to Union Island to reunite with his family, and a young lady named Edith Mulrain, who was the love of his life. In 1910, his dream almost came true when he left America on a ship to the Caribbean. He had even bought an engagement ring for Edith. Unfortunately, his journey home was significantly derailed in Jamaica when he lost his clothes, the engagement ring, and every penny that he had earned during his years away from Union Island. As a result, he was forced back into the tentacles of America, where he had to start life all over again. The question is: Why did he not return to Union Island nonetheless?

In 1912 his younger brother James, who was 18 years

old, migrated to America to join him. Then in the years 1914, Lavina, his sister, at age 24, also left Union Island to accompany them. They all lived together at Hugh's residence in Maryland. What remains difficult to understand is that although these youngsters had come from a well-to-do family, and had a good life, after they left, they never returned to Union Island to call it home again. Many other Unionites likewise left and never returned. So the logical question that must be asked is, what is that influence or gravitational force that has such an impact on many Unionites whenever they venture abroad? "Do they became enamored and later tethered by the sudden niceties of their new environments? Or do they choose migration as a means of escaping the bleakness of life in Union Island?"

It is reputed that four of Hugh's other siblings, Edward, Irvin, Una, Lamie, and his mother Ada later migrated to America. May, his last sister was the only one that remained in Union Island throughout her entire life. In her latter years, she was fondly called Mother May.

There isn't any detailed information regarding the whereabouts of Charles Mulzac's other three children: Mary, John and Emma, except that John (Johnnie) once ran his father's rum shop. Therefore, the current generations of the Mulzac's family that live in Union Island and bear the family name "Mulzac" are descendants of the above. Edward, the second son of Richard Mulzac was the father of the late Leonard Mulzac, (Dogma) a life-long resident of Union Island. There may also be descendants of Irvin Mulzac, the younger brother of Hugh. While still living in Union Island, Irvin buried his dad Richard at Ashton Cemetery on February 14, 1930.

It was only during his latter years (1960's), that Hugh Mulzac returned to St. Vincent with the intention to settle. Why did he make up his mind at such a late stage in his life? During his sojourn in St. Vincent, he gave multiple lectures and classes in the art of painting. He also exhibited to local yachtsmen the vast knowledge and experience he attained at sea while in Europe and North America. Regrettably, Hugh's stay in the region was short-lived. He returned to America soon thereafter.

Among Unionites living abroad, men make up the larger percentage of the ones who wish to return home permanently. Women on the other hand, are more adaptive to their new environments and are willing to settle almost anywhere with their families.

But is there a right time to return permanently to Union Island to satisfy that nostalgic yearning? If so, when?

Andy Kwame Stewart, a native of Union Island thinks that if anyone has that burning desire to return permanently to Union, then he or she should just pickup and leave. "The temptations in America are enormous," he states. "No one really gets into that ideal state of mind to leave permanently; and before you know it, you are already feeble." "Do not wait," he exhorted, "the time will **never** be just right."

It is approximately a century now since Unionites have been migrating steadily to other countries. During the first half of the 20th century when Unionites were venturing out in droves, their primary purpose was for employment. Although employment remains an essential reason for today's migration, there are a myriad of other necessities that can only be attained via migration. And regrettably, most of these necessities can only be attained abroad.

The percentage of returning Unionites is insignificant compared to those who make these foreign countries their homes. Currently, there is a large concentration of Unionites in America, Canada, UK, and Trinidad & Tobago notwithstanding the many that are scattered throughout the globe. In recent years, Unionites have been setting up homes on the island of St. Vincent. But St. Vincent is located only 40 miles north of Union Island. So again, why? Now it must be observed that in recent times, it is the younger members of the families that leave the island for greener pastures. And whenever any resident of Union Island leaves the island for that purpose, there is only a slender possibility that they will return to call Union Island home. Often they leave their parents and grandparents behind. They at some point become parents themselves, their children are born outside of Union Island for sure, which leaves the island with a low percentage of births from the original Unionite population. The numbers are surely dwindling quickly while the island is facing a massive brain drain.

So what really is The Exodus Factor? Is it a custom, a legacy, an established system in Union island in which migration has become inevitable? Is it the status quo that a better life is easily attainable abroad, where multiple opportunities abound as opposed to the limitations of the region? This significant question will be answered in many ways, long before the final page of this book is turned.

If a survey were to be conducted on every home in Union island, commencing from the last house at Campbell, Ashton, which was owned by the late Presol Ambrose (Presey) to the first house at Point Lookout, Clifton, many would be amazed. It would be astounding to realize that each home on that island has at least one member of its family that has left the island permanently. For other families, the parents are the only ones left at home. The members of the families who have left are now living abroad, or on another island in the region. Does this indicate that there is a dislike for this beautiful Caribbean paradise? Absolutely not! For this is also evident in other Caribbean countries. For Union Island, many will tacitly agree that migration has become the inevitable.

On Sunday, October 27, 2013, the author had reason to visit a funeral service that was held at the Seventh Day Adventist Church at Ashton, Union Island. There, he met with one of the local minister named Aldon Ambrose. They had a protracted discussion about the scenery, childhood days, and the changes that the island has encountered over the years. But they could not sidestep the fact that every member of that family, beside the parents was living outside of Union Island. To commiserate with their sobbing father, and be a part of that funeral service, every sibling of the family had to return to Union Island from their distant homes. This again is not exclusive to this family, for it has become status quo on Union Island, unfortunately.

Minister Ambrose mentioned that he observed this unforgiving trend several years ago when he returned to Union Island from Canada to visit his parents. " I was literally shocked, "he said. "As a result, I made it a concerted effort to leave Canada for a while in order to accompany my parents who were literally living alone."

Fortunately, for the many that have migrated abroad to improve their lives, a significant number of them have made good of the opportunities available to them. In some cases, they have made sacrifices to obtain those opportunities. Many of them are now doctors, judges, lawyers, engineers, professors, bankers, accountants, nurses, schoolteachers, principals, building contractors, and a host of other professionals from a myriad of other disciplines.

Let us now take a look at a scenario of a family who has migrated to the Americas or Europe.

Today an average family in Union Island entails a mother and father and their four children. A dearth of academic opportunities on the Island would only engender migration at some time in the early lives of the children. Because that has become the inevitable as mentioned previously, the authenticity of the original culture of Union Island is notably declining. These children who migrate to other countries for economic and academic reasons are apt to have their parents with them at some point in time. The lifestyles in those countries are different; their parents are quick to point that out after they have lived out their novelty stage. They complain about their confinements in homes where doors are bolted with two or three locks, windows are shut tightly, and radiators are going constantly to maintain heat during the horrid winter months. Another downside to this is that people's mobility is grossly compromised by a 180-degree turn from the previous walking habit they enjoyed over the many years spent in Union Island.

One can only imagine the health issues that stem from not being able to do the things that were once enjoyed. Nevertheless, this New atmosphere and environment has become their homes, and in most cases, their abode.

While youngsters sometimes assimilate very well into their new environment, their patents, on the other hand struggle with their new lifestyle. They are persuaded and in some cases, coerced into dwellings that are far removed from their true definition of home in Union Island. A trip or two back home is quite in order for the parents, but that is about it, for they later return to the unfamiliar lifestyle of Europe and the Americas. The opportunity to meet, greet, and converse on a daily basis with neighbors has dissipated. Older folks have genuine respect for their peers, so neighbors in their new environments will not hesitate to extend hospitality. But the sad thing is that the neighborly customs of America, Canada, and Europe differs immensely from the customs of the Caribbean as a whole.

27

Nostalgia becomes evident, while boredom and stress seeps in quickly. These of course, are cogent ingredients for accelerated aging. A final request by the parents to be sent back home permanently often falls on the obstinate ears of their children. Boredom, stress, and depression continue as the end approaches.

This is basically the trend of today's generations. Many are of the belief that in the next two decades, the population of the indigenous Unionites will dwindle its way into insignificance. Many have witnessed the dead being buried on whatever turf they end up on; their bodies are seldom sent back home for burial at the local cemeteries. Nevertheless, life in Union Island will continue amidst the constant evolution. Above all, it must be acknowledged that the Exodus Factor is there to stay.

◆◆◆□*Chapter Two*

AN INSIDE LOOK

Union Island, with its peaks such as Mr. Parnassus, Mt. Tabor, Mt. Campbell, and Mt. Olympus, is by far the most mountainous of all the Grenadines Islands, which makes hiking a must in this rocky terrain. Approximately three miles long and one mile wide (4.54 square miles) with a meager population of approximately 4,500, Union Island is made up of two villages, Ashton and Clifton, which Samuel Spann named after his hometown of Bristol, England. Ashton, the larger of the two villages, consists of Ashton Village, Campbell, Valley, Bordeaux, Garden Field, Dominique, Bonnet, Richmond, Belmont, Jerome, Chatham, Ms. Pierre (Ms. Pay), and Ms. Irene. Areas such as Campbell, Ms. Pierre, and Ms. Irene attained their names from native females who once farmed these lands during the famous cotton era. The district of Campbell was called Ms. Campbell until recent years.

Clifton, on the other hand, consists of Point Lookout, Clifton Village, Moure, Downson, Penfield, Cotton, and so on. Having such small landmass makes Union Island one of the most densely populated small islands in the region, but it does not appear that way because there are still numerous acres of lands that are uncultivated.

The rocky terrain of this little island is much more pronounced than that of her sister islands throughout the Grenadines. Mt. Tabor, at an altitude one foot short of officially being called a mountain, is not the only conspicuous peak that grasps a visitor's attention. Mt. Olympus and her sister peak, Mt. Parnassus, (locally called Big Hill), cannot escape the gazing eyes of any first-time visitor to the island.

These two peaks are both a smidgen lower than Mt. Tabor. Mt. Parnassus, which overlooks the central village of Ashton, may appear alarmingly precarious to a first-time visitor.

Mt. Olympus; looks like a cone projecting out of a volcanic crater.

However, its bold presence is not a deterrent to any of the residents whose parents and grandparents have lived their entire lives looking up at it. A visitor noted, some thirty-five years ago, that the first time she was driven to Ashton, she felt timid, as she got closer to this huge hill, which appeared as though it was moving aggressively toward her. However, she said, after visiting the island time and time again, "It is like a different kettle of fish. Mt. Tabor is part of a range of highland that runs in a westerly direction that ends at a peak of dense vegetation named Mt. Campbell.

Many of these highpoints proved to be good lookout sites against enemies. Numerous cannons are still intact at key points throughout the island. These archaic weapons are rather eye-catching to tourists, who seize every opportunity to visit these locations, take pictures, and make historical documentation where necessary. Bloody Bay, which is situated on the northern coast of the island, speaks of the massive bloodshed associated with that particular region during maritime wars. Is it the blood of the original settlers of Union Island, the Amerindians? Sure it is! Did they not fight to their bitter end when the French first lay feet on the island to claim their land? To date, there is no historical documentation available to indicate their total debacle. Yet available to the people of Union Island, is the history of the Henry Morgan. What a shame!

From an aerial view of St. Vincent and the Grenadines, one cannot escape the picturesque beauty that lies beneath. The long spans of reefs that engulf the white sandy beaches are enticing not only to the marine biologists, and anglers but also to the average visitor. Amazingly, there are also hot springs—underwater volcanoes with continuous bubbles. The water temperature changes dramatically, becoming very warm at times. Also present is an abundance of outstanding corals in this vast expanse of reefs.

Boat-racing, snorkeling, spear fishing, waterskiing, game fishing, yachting, scuba diving in shallow water, and other aquatic sports are just a few of the enormous marine activities and attractions that exist on the island. Diving in these pristine territories offers opportunities to capture a panoramic submarine view and coexist with marine creatures such as the Frog Fish, Nurse Shark, Octopus (locally called the Sea Cat), Barracuda, Stingray, Manta Ray, Porcupine Fish, Congo Eel, Green Eel, Christmas-Tree Worm, and many others that inhabit the underwater world.

On Grenadinesdive.com are some pictures of the pristine underwater elegance in the confines of St. Vincent and the Grenadines. The famed diver, Glenroy Adams has captured and brought the elegance of the marine ecology at our fingertips.

Multiple land animals are residents of Union Island; fortunately none of them are venomous. There are well over forty species of intriguing birds dispersed throughout the island. Some can be found at the seashore, in swamps, in pastures, and amid the dense vegetation inland. The **Green-Throated Carib**, locally called the Hummingbird, is the smallest specie known. It can be seen extracting the juices of flowers during the ephemeral rainy season. The largest of the birds is the **Brown Pelican**. This excellent diver is seen mainly in the air and sea, and in most cases is accompanied by its marine counterpart, the **Laughing Gull** (David) another excellent diver that follows fishermen out at sea. Wherever fish abound in the sea, these predatory birds are found in clusters. This Brown Pelican, locally called the Gramazier, is edible and is sometimes hunted for its meat.

The **Belted Kingfisher**, another native bird, has characteristics similar to those of the aforementioned birds. This bird can be seen mainly at the shallow coastal waters. The **Carib**

Grackle, or black bird, is quite an intriguing character to contend with; the detail of how this menace operates is the subject of a later chapter. Another bird that children were warned to keep their distance from is the **Grey Kingbird**. This one is locally called the Pickery. It earns this name from its willingness to ward off any potential threat, even humans. During its breeding season, this bird is exceptionally aggressive toward anything that ventures near its path. It is extremely protective of its eggs or young ones. The **Zenaida dove** (mountain dove), Rameau, and Ground dove belong to the same species of doves. The Rameau is the largest of the dove family in Union Island. Its proper name is the **Scaly-Naped** pigeon, and like the rest of the doves, it is adorned with beautiful feathers. This bird though, is blue and has bright red eyes. It can be seen only on tall trees or in the highlands. During the onset of flight, the wings of these regal birds exude a melodious sound.

The **Tropical Mockingbird**, similar in size to the Grey Kingbird, is locally called the Packer Chin Chay. During the late 1970s, this was one of the most proliferous birds found on Union Island. On the numerous Kashie trees (thorny tree) of Campbell, they were found hovering in huge fleets. The **Cattle Egrets** are white, lanky, long-legged birds that share the grassy pastures with cattle. Because they prey on insects and other vertebrates that are parasites to these larger animals, they are sometimes seen standing on the backs of these hosts.

The **Rufous vented Chachalaca** are very timid and wild and seldom seen, except in the dense vegetation of Queensbury, Colon Campbell, and so forth. This brown bird that resembles the domestic fowl also has some notable characteristics similar to those of the turkey. It is locally called the Cocorico and is the national bird of Trinidad and Tobago. The **Osprey** is a huge predator that almost all other birds on the island fear. The locals call it the chicken hawk. Whenever a domestic fowl is frantically seeking cover, there is a probability that a hovering Osprey is nearby. Other birds of the island include the Smooth-billed Ani (Jumbee Bird), the Black-faced Grass Quit, (Cheridee), the Banana Quit, Wilson Plover, Green-throated Carib, Green Heron, Caribbean Martin, Bare-eyed Thrush, Magnificent Frigate (scissors), and a host of other eye-catching feathered creatures.

Two species of snakes are native to Union Island: the **Tree Boa** (congo) and **Grass snake** (Black snakes). The colorful

Congo snake is the larger of the two and looks very much like a python. This nocturnal reptile is extremely lazy and can be found wrapped up like the shape of a ball, sleeping on the branches of a low tree. In pursuit of its prey, this animal moves slowly but gingerly, aided by its gift of camouflage. The Congo snake grows to an average length of four feet. The Black snake on the other hand is shorter and much slenderer. Although called black, the true color of this adult snake is dark brown, but its underside is bright white. This agile creature grows to a length of approximately 32 inches. Unlike its larger counterpart that sleeps openly on trees the Black snake's home is mainly in the holes of large trees. Both reptiles are nonvenomous and very timid by nature. They can be seen in the dense bushes and highlands rather than on the lower coastal
region. To date, there has never been an incident of snakebite on the island. They both feed on lizards, snails, and other small vertebrates.

The opossum, called Manicou by the natives, is an animal that was hunted for its meat during the earlier years, dating back to the Amerindians. It was once considered a menace to farmers with large flocks of domestic chickens (fowl). Over the years, the lifestyle of the natives has changed so significantly that today there is seldom any chickens raised at home for meat or eggs. The hunting of this dog-like animal has long been a thing of the past. Other than humans, it has no known predators, and as a result, its population is expected to increase bountifully.

Like the armadillo, the tastiest of all wild meats, the opossum was once considered a delicacy in Union Island. But unlike this swift creature that is hunted during broad daylight, the opossum was hunted during the midnight and early hours of the morning. The flambeau or Massantow were the only sources of light for hunters through the entire course of this nocturnal mission.

Manicou are prevalent during the rainy season when the Manicou apple trees are laden with ripened fruits. But Manicou apples are not the only food that makes up their diet, for they would not resist the temptation to feast on the local fowl that sleep on trees during the night. This seldom happens, but whenever it does, a cornucopia of noise erupts from the rest of the birds, which are forced to leave the comfort of their resting place to the ground beneath.

Dogs have always been man's help, man's best friend, and so these animals have been an integral part of hunting. On a good night of hunting, three young men, each with his own dog, would descend on every Manicou apple tree in the vicinity. The hairy Manicou, on seeing the lights and hearing the sounds of their vicious predators, become intensely nervous and immediately seek cover in the highest branches of the trees or on the ground. Those that seek refuge on the ground are at the mercy of the carnivorous jaws that await them. A climber can also shake to the ground those that make the higher branches their sanctuary; they eventually become victims too. The almost lifeless catch is then taken into a holding bag, preferably the caucus bag. The hunters visit a few more trees, or even revisit the same tree, causing the catch to grow in number.

At the end of the hunt, the catch is taken to one of the hunters' homes, where a fire is lit and the fur is cleanly burned off the skin. The animals are then cut open and gutted. Special parts of the animals are cut off and given to each dog for his hard work. These parts are areas of the endocrine system, such as the groin, testicles, glands, feet, and other parts that are said to stimulate the dog's aggression during hunting. The huge catch is divided equally among the hunters, who then disperse and head to their respective homes, where the bulk of meat is then cut to pieces, washed, and seasoned. One of the condiments used is local thyme, which is called Big Thyme. This herb has great medicinal value that will be explained in a later chapter. Fresh sea salt, which is harvested from a local salt pond, is also used. The abundant fresh wild meat is cooked and devoured within a few days. Refrigerators were only a dream, of course, in the past.

The iguana is another animal that abounds in the rocky terrain of this mountainous cay. An adult iguana is much larger than the opossum, its counterpart. This reptile can be seen lurking on the brink of rocks during the early evening hours, or even on rocks overhanging the sea. As the old saying by Dr. Amos N. Wilson claims, "Power is a chameleon; it takes on the texture of its environment." These multicolored reptiles are exceptionally adaptable everywhere. Like the opossum, the meat of this reptilian wonder is also edible; everyone tends to associate its taste with that of chicken. The skin of the opossum is burnt in a light fire before it is gutted, clean and season. By tradition, the meat of this animal is seldom eaten by the natives.

The Tropical Mocking bird (Packer Chin-Chin)

Hotels, Restaurant, Bars

ANCHORAGE YACHT CLUB

Making your way across the Caribbean blue waters of the Grenadines takes you into a whole new realm. You have arrived at The Anchorage Yacht Club on Union Island, a casual and comfortable hotel along the white beaches of the crystal clear turquoise waters of Clifton lagoon, far away from the mass tourism. The exotic romance continues with the resort's accommodation – all our rooms are waterfront, some on the first floor with a panoramic view over the marina from a spacious balcony; the rest is directly on the white sand of the beach.

Union Island has a wide choice of restaurants, whether you look for a fast lunch or a romantic lobster dinner. Here are all the restaurants known on Union Island. The nightlife on Union isn't huge, but it has a special Caribbean vibe. What better way to end your day than with a rum and coke or beer listening to reggae tunes and looking at the sunset...

CAPTAIN GOURMET

Run by a French couple, Captain Gourmet is the place to be every morning to enjoy the best breakfast or brunch in the Grenadines. You will find different kind of coffees, French croissants and baguettes, or you can also choose the amazing breakfast with eggs, bacon, tomatoes, spring rolls, etc. In the mean time you can use the free Wi-Fi and see what's going on around the world.

ANCHORAGE RESTAURANT

If you are staying at the Anchorage Yacht Club, how convenient to come out of your room and have lunch or dinner next to the famous shark pool! The Anchorage restaurant serves pizzas, meat, lobster and delicious fresh fish. It also has a bar, free Wi-Fi and a beautiful view over the lagoon. The Anchorage bar is a nice place to relax after a kite or surf session. Sit next to the shark pool and enjoy the view while enjoying an excellent colorful cocktail.

BOUGAINVILLA RESTAURANT

Next to the Anchorage you will find the lovely Bougainvilla hotel, bar and restaurant. The restaurant has a lot of choice; my personal favorite is the fresh sashimi with the secret sauce. The surroundings with the huge, beautiful aquarium and the view of the lagoon make it a romantic place to have lunch or dinner. Bougainvilla has a friendly staff and tasty drinks. You can enjoy a drink at the bar while your food is getting ready.

CIAO MARIE

Marie's restaurant is a very charming little restaurant next to the square in Clifton. Marie is French and an excellent chef. Fish, pastas or pizza, it is a great place to go after a full days kite session, the portions are generous and you always eat very well.

THE WEST INDIES

The West Indies is a reference in the Grenadines when it comes to good food. Joel will be happy to welcome you and tell you more about the life on Union island. She is French and knows abut good cuisine and serves various dishes with fish and meat. The meat is especially good there.

LAMBI

If you are looking for a more traditional restaurant with a steel band playing during your dinner, Lambi is for you, they will serve you all the local dishes with the traditional music playing.

CHATHAM – SECKIE & VANESSA

On the beach of Chatham bay, Seckie & Vanessa will welcome you to this typical shack right on the beach. They will cook you all the traditional food with lobsters and fish. You cannot walk from Clifton to Chatham (unless you want to walk for an hour). If you are planning on eating there we advice you to reserve in advance.

T & N AT NOLA's

I challenge you to finish your plate at Nola's! She cooks tasty local food, carrying in more coming every time you think you are done, no guest is leaving Nola hungry.

BIG SAND – DOGGY's

Located on Big sand beach and open for lunch every day, you can have a drink or eat with the beautiful view of the blue ocean and white beach.

JENNIFER'S

On the way to Ashton Village, climbing the hill you will find Jennifer's restaurant on the right, she cooks very nice chicken and fish with a variation of fresh, local vegetables. The food can take some time but you will not be disappointed by the result.

JOY'S

Open every Friday and Saturday night, Joy cooks some of the best barbecue chicken on the island.

TWILIGHT

Twilight is a bar but they also serve fast food. Keep on drinking and order some of the burgers with fries or a plate of samosas.

LAMBI

For one of the cheapest and fastest lunches in town, Lambi is where you want to go. The lunch boxes are ready and you can pick yours up for 8EC$. In the box you will find rice or macaroni together with fried fish, chicken or roasted turkey.

BIG CITY

Union Island's favorite fast food is Big City. Located upstairs of the Tourist Bureau, you can choose from a wide and addictive daily menu. You can eat there or take it away. They serve chicken, conch shells, corn, potatoes, rice pasta, hamburgers, fish etc.…

The food is served very fast; it is very good and at a very affordable price!

EAGLE'S NEST

Eagle nest makes some very good roti every Thursday. The roti is a local wrap stuffed with meat, chicken or conch, together with vegetables. One is enough to keep you full the whole day.

ICE CREAM PLACE

The ice cream shop might be the cutest business on the island. In the middle of Clifton's fruit market, the ice cream shop is shaped like colorful wooden boat. They have many different kinds of refreshing ice creams and milk shakes.

HAPPY ISLAND

Renown worldwide for its originality, Happy Island is the first ever bar built on a conch shell base in the middle of the lagoon of Clifton. You can access this charming little bar by taxi boat or with your own dingy. Facing the west you can enjoy the sunset every day with a glass of Genty's famous rum punch.

TWILIGHT

Twilight is where you want to start your evening, or even finish it if you feel like it. The bar opens early, which allow everyone to have a few drinks before dinner. We often end up staying there, skipping dinner and partying. They often have live bands and local music playing. The place is small but the ambience is great, and everyone always have a good time in twilight.

CRUISER'S BAR

A cool lounge with good music playing and a wide choice of good cocktails.

GREEN LIGHT BAR

The local bar plays some of the best reggae, dancehall and soca music in the Caribbean. Cheap drinks to a Caribbean rhythm.

Courtesy kitesurfgrenacines.com

Union Island Airport

The year 1974 marked the birth of the long-awaited Union Island Airport at Point Lookout, Clifton. Mr. Andre Beaufrand, the entrepreneurial mastermind who constructed this once private airport, was of French origin. This airbase now replaces a coral reef, a mangrove marshland, and a very tiny island known as Red Island. Unionites know this little rock as Mancheuse. The mangrove lowland was once the breathing ground for crabs, which were hunted regularly for local dishes and, to a lesser extent, marketing. Natives regularly visited the large coral reef and shallow water that spanned throughout the western part of Point Lookout Beach to collect numerous whelks, crustaceans, and conch, a luscious delicacy in the region.

During the late 1970s and 1980s, Union Island Airport was one of the busiest airports in the Caribbean. Although, at that time the airport was half its current size, it was home to numerous airplanes that landed almost every twenty minutes. Today, even though there are many touchdowns from numerous countries, the airport is far from what it used to be some three decades ago; there has been a drastic reduction in the air traffic over the years.

There is the St. Vincent & the Grenadines Airways (SVG Airways) that conduct regular daily flights between St. Vincent and the Grenadines islands—Bequia, Canouan, and Union Island. LIAT is another airline that takes passengers from Barbados to St. Vincent & the Grenadines and to Grenada via the regional islands. There once was a tiny landing base on Palm Island (neighboring Cay) before the Union Island Airport was built. This was a boon to the resort there, facilitating tourism in the region. Palm Island is one of the hidden treasures of the Grenadines that possesses a resort that is second to none.

The airstrip of Union Island was expanded in 1995 to accommodate larger aircraft. The terminal was relocated, and a host of modern facilities were set in place. Then in May of 2009, a major restoration project was conducted. This process was scheduled in two phases. The first phase entailed asphalt resurfacing of the runway, taxiway, an apron (an area of almost 250,000 sq. feet), pavement marking, and minor landscaping of the area.

The second phase placed rock armoring toward the western end of the landing strip to increase the protection of the newly renovated infrastructure. Although this process was swiftly executed by CCA Limited, the airport was unfortunately rendered out of commission, but only for a short period of time.

Today with the availability of landing bases in these seemingly remote vicinities, the Grenadines islands are easily accessible at the click of a mouse.

Aerial view of Union Island's Airstrip. Located at Clifton

FRIGATE ISLAND (ROCK)

Frigate Island is a very small, uninhabited island that is situated approximately 3/4 mile off the northern coast of Union Island. The name Frigate Rock will be used for the remainder of this book. It is the only term used by Unionites to refer to this small island.

Although Union Island is a separate landmass from the neighboring cay, Frigate Rock, these two were always regarded as one. Perhaps the two cays were connected to each other centuries ago. Not too long ago, residents used to walk the shallow reef that separated Union Island from this nearby four-acre landmass. Walking was much easier during low tide than when the water level was higher. This reef was called "Grass" and was home to many crustaceans. The conch and sea urchin, both native to this reef, were hunted and eaten as a delicacy. The presence of "Grass" may be a clear reminder that this presumably single landmass had been eroded centuries ago.

As Hugh Mulzac mentioned in A Star to Steer By, someone could walk out into the sea for a mile or more in water no deeper than your waist. One can observe a sudden 90-degree drop from the southern part of Union Island that is closest to Frigate Rock (in the vicinity of the late Meldon John's house, of Campbell). This area is arguably 40 feet or more above sea level and has shown evidence of water erosion in the past, and erosion is still evident today. In that area, lots of boulders can be found in the sea.

The Ashton Cemetery that lies along the coastline and opposite of Frigate Rock has also fallen victim to the advancing sea. This severe erosion over a prolonged period has resulted in many human bones or fossils becoming visible along the shoreline. In the mid-1970s, a construction project was conducted at that site to prevent further erosion. The use of wire baskets filled with boulders has been laid along the shoreline. As a result, there was no evidence of further erosion.

Frigate Island from a northwesterly view. A partial view of Petit Martinique is seen at the rear.

Frigate Rock is currently uninhabited. Yet approximately 30 percent of this small island is flat and is suitable for a tourist resort. For many decades, tourists have used the sheltered water of this island as a docking port for their yachts and the calm waters for skiing. Like Fort Charlotte in the mainland of St. Vincent, Frigate Rock had been used to house the African Negroes who were afflicted with yaws and leprosy many, many years ago. They were separated from the rest of society but were cared for and encouraged to bathe regularly in the sea. Bathing in the sea was widely encouraged because the high saline content was believed to bring salutary results.

During those earlier years, leprosy, which causes deformities of the face and extremities, was somewhat prevalent in these geographical areas, but is almost nonexistent today. It is believed that this leprosy, or Hansen's disease, is spread via respiratory droplets. Studies have shown that it can be transmitted to humans via armadillos that harbor the Mycobacterium Leprae, the causative agent. The Armadillo is an animal with very sharp claws that digs for its food. It also carries a very strong armor that protects it from predators. The meat of this animal is considered the tastiest of wild meats in Trinidad and Tobago. This animal was introduced to St. Vincent by way of Grenada a few years ago. It is said that these animals are multiplying very rapidly in the Greggs and Richland Park areas of the mainland (St. Vincent) and are in the initial stage of becoming an agricultural menace. Nevertheless, armadillos are nowhere to be found in Union Island. Leprosy is seldom seen nowadays in the Caribbean.

Yaws, on the other hand, is a very contagious disease that affects the skin and can penetrate all the way to the bone. This disease, which is also known as Frambesia, is of tropical origin. It was prevalent in Africa, South America, East Asia, and the Caribbean. Fortunately, this disease, which also causes deformities of the face and skin, can be easily treated with a single dose of antibiotics.

It is prudent to surmise that Dr. H. Nichols' (American doctor) presence on Union Island on Tuesday, June 11, 1891, was not by accident but to treat those who were affected by these contagious ailments. During his visit, he was appalled by the deplorable conditions that afflicted the Africans on the plantation. He later expressed the distastefulness of his observation.

Obed, the son of Ann Edwards (Ma Dee), an old woman from Clifton village, was afflicted with leprosy, an unforgiving disorder, and hence became a resident of Frigate Rock. There was little that Ma Dee could have done for her beloved son regarding the condition of his health. Nevertheless, she was satisfied that she had the opportunity to send food, clothes, and anything edible to him. She knew ahead of time that a fishing boat was heading in the direction of Frigate Rock the following morning. That night she prepared a roasted coconut bake, and early the next morning when the boat was leaving, she handed a package containing the bake to one of the crew. "Give meh son this bake for meh please," she uttered in the dialect of that day. Delighted that she was able to do something worthwhile for her son, she knew very well that he, too, would appreciate such a gesture of his mother's love.

She immediately ran off from the beach where the boat had just left for its destination, and up she went to the highland where the Catholic Church is situated (a current landmark). There she stood as the boat made its way through the reefs and shallow areas into deeper waters. Ma Dee was alert and watchful, as the little craft got closer to Frigate Rock. Unable to contain her excitement, she began to wave at the fishermen as though they would be able to see her from such distance. Her excitement quickly turned to gloom, and finally into anger, as she watched the boat slowly sail by the island.

Immediately she began to bawl loudly, expressing her hurt and dissatisfaction. Her inconsolable sobbing instantly caught the attention of lots of people in the community—a community so small that everyone literally knew each other fairly well. By midday, everyone was quite aware of the heinous crime committed—that of neglecting to deliver the mother's gifts to her son. Such a crime, of course, was not tolerated in the close-knit community, where cohesiveness was always the order of the day.

On returning from their fishing trip, these sailors did not see any reason to visit Frigate Rock. They had already devoured the contents of the package (coconut bake) on their long day at sea. That afternoon, residents expressed their displeasure by physically beating members of the crew to make an example out of them and to assuage the pain of the aggrieved mother.

Frigate Rock also used to be a lookout point for the local fishermen of Union Island. They climbed the higher region of the small island, where they could have a panoramic view of the fishes' movements from the deeper water to the shallow, westerly side of the island. Jack fish can be seen from a distance, for they appear very dark in the lighter blue waters. These smaller fish being chased by the larger predatory fishes swim into the shallow lagoon-like area for rescue. It was from the pinnacle of Frigate Rock that a local fisherman called David John, aka Gayman, would bellow at the top of his lungs, "Fish-oooooooh," alerting other fishermen on Union Island that there were fish to be caught. The waiting fishermen, with their seines on board, would then hastily roar their boats to the location of the fish. Meticulously watching the movement of the fish while in ready position, the fishermen would seize the first opportunity and cast their huge nets in hopes of engulfing their prize.

The young fishermen of Union Island seldom practice this fine art of fishing. Instead, spearfishing is more prevalent today. If the fish were caught about a hundred yards from the shoreline, the fishermen would decide to haul the catch ashore. Because news got around so quickly, numerous young men would rush to the site of the catch to lend a hand in pulling the prize ashore. On completion of this process, everyone was guaranteed to leave with a small portion of the catch, which made his evening's effort worthwhile.

In the early 1990s, the government of St. Vincent and the Grenadines made a gallant attempt to construct a 300-boat marina at Frigate Rock and Ashton Harbor. This was deemed a practical endeavor to generate income in the region and to create employment and economic stability on Union Island. While the project was in full swing, it did made vehicular transportation viable to and from the two neighboring cays. It is reputed that the French company that procured this major project went into receivership, and the project came to a crashing halt. Although this major undertaking was designed to generate a newfound income in the region, it did affect the ecology in the nearby mangrove region of Union Island quite negatively. The abandoned project has blocked the bay's circulation, causing the water of the eastern region of Ashton harbor to become stagnated and murky. Conch, lobsters, corals, and all sorts of fish have been destroyed. A venerated grunt fishing ground was totally destroyed during the construction of this major marine project. This fishing ground was located midway to the Frigate Rock, lining up with Sail Rock at its easterly lower point; only the seasoned fisherman of today will remember profoundly the site where these grunts were once plentiful.

The seawater at the most easterly end of Ashton Harbor and Top Yonder Bay has become stagnated since the project began," said one resident. "The saline content at that area has been severely compromised," he added. The narrow water passage between Union Island and Frigate Rock is no more. Small crafts can no longer use this shortcut in and out of Ashton Harbor; instead they have to circumnavigate the entire cay of Frigate Rock to and from their requisite destinations. The shoreline at the Ashton Cemetery shows no further threat of erosion; rather, it has a renewed beach from the copious deposits of sand. The negative side of that is that the influx of sand in that region has smothered and destroyed the coral reef and sea grass, resulting in further ecological damage to the fish, lobsters, and conch population.

At the turn of the twentieth century, Frigate Rock and the famed Top Yonder Bay were shipbuilding sites for the respected Mulzac family. They were adept at this craft, and it is out of this legacy that Union Island produced some of the best shipwrights in the region—Eastman Stewart, Gurry Stewart, Solomon Stewart, Incoman Stewart, Paul Wilson, Percival Thomas (Brother Tom), Sonny Wilson, and Tanil Sandy. Even the soon-to-be centenarian, Augustus King Mitchell, did his share of shipbuilding during his formative years. These men actually built and launched their boats at Top Yonder Bay.

Frigate Rock was also a huge getaway site on most weekends, and the home of some huge whelks too. Residents frequented the sandy coastal lowlands of this little cay to have their regular picnics. Elaborate cooking for those local events was done at home ahead of time. Pelau was often the dish of choice on these occasions. Pelau is a very tasty dish made primarily on weekends and especially when family and friends get together on special occasions— to "lime" as is said in the local parlances of the Caribbean. The main components of this dish are rice, green pigeon peas, and goat meat. Sadly, much of these communal activities have declined over the years. Frigate Rock's receptive arms still remain just a few minutes away from the harbor of Ashton. A rowboat might just be the ideal vehicle.

EVOLUTION

Looking back at the island two generations age, one can affirm with absolute certainty that the island has changed drastically along the shorelines. There was once a small rock that extended out of Basin Beach. There is no sign of it today; it was completely eroded by the constantly incoming waves. The once-huge expanses of land that make up Basin and its adjacent beaches have eroded considerably into a sharp V-shaped projection. This area was once called "Sand," and its projection along the coastline "Queensbury Point."

Earlier maps of Union Island clearly show the extent of the erosion caused by the encroaching sea. The coastline west of Basin Beach is another visible site of erosion; numerous boulders lay along the shoreline some three hundred feet while the land immediately above still bears a near sixty-degree drop. This is a clear indication that that portion of the land faced erosion many years before. The coastal area that was easily accessible by foot some forty years ago has become almost impossible to walk on because of the encroachment of the sea.

In "Sand," numerous local grape trees and coconut palms were once a major part of its lush vegetation. Today, a few rotten trunks, mark the presence of a once-flourishing coconut plantation; some of them can now be seen in the water. On the other hand, a few grape trees are still there, though sparse compared to earlier years. Among the coconuts palms formerly in this region, residents of Ashton Village once occupied individual plots of land that they cultivated with sand-potatoes, or Puddocks. Older folks are familiar with the name Puddocks. These potatoes are in Union Island and maybe the other Grenadine islands.

Sand potatoes are primarily white and small, 1/2 the size of the regular sweet potatoes. They are very tasty, especially because of the high salt content in the sandy soil, as opposed to that of the lands of higher altitudes.

Erosion, as alluded to earlier, has indeed proven its dominance over any natural accretion on the beaches. Everyone remembers the beautiful white sandy beach called Top Yonder Bay; this little harbor became the principal shipyard on the island, dating back to the Mulzac's era. The last of the local vessels were built and launched on that site. One notable vessel that was built and launched at this site was Prince Louisa, which was owned by August King Mitchell. This location was also where some of the largest festivals (boat launching) took place; it was where the African culture came alive with the beat of the Big Drum (African Drum). Alas, Top Yonder Bay is now a thing of the past.

On any Sunday afternoon, the famous beach would have been filled to its capacity with residents enjoying a sea bath. The affinity of this beach to the Ashton Village makes it easily accessible for nearby residents.

The Mangrove marshland that partially engulfs this beach has been moving inward for many years now. The marine project of Frigate Rock that was mentioned earlier may have contributed partially to this unfavorable outcome. For someone to get to this beach, the best practical route would be water transport.

Forty years ago, vehicles drove from Ashton Jetty through the salt pond and on to Big Tamarind (a significant landmark on Clifton Road) to get to Clifton. The salt pond was solid land, then, and void of the large expanse of mangrove vegetation that now exists. The Easter Festival of 1979 marked one of the largest sporting events that had ever happened on Union Island, and it took place at the Ashton Salt Pond. Cricket, a notable sport; was played there. The Union Island Secondary School had its own Cricket team during the 1970s. In 1975-76, the team competed with the Hillsborough Secondary School of Carriacou at the Ashton Salt Pond. Two years earlier, it had competed with them at Hillsborough, Carriacou.

With the loss of the principal cricket field, playing ground, and a few beaches at the hands of the encroaching mangrove and sea, Union Island have regressed quite a bit. From a sporting perspective, surely the island is not better today than it was forty years ago.

Chapter Three

WE THING

New accents are formed when people of a different country and tongue learn another language. As slaves from West Africa were brought to Union Island, they were forced to learn European languages, but they were not entirely successful at mastering the languages. To date, the African influence is much more predominant in Union Island, even after many years of colonization. Obviously, as with anything new, there were challenges, and in this case, challenges in pronunciation that resulted in a myriad variance of words. Most of these variants were pronounced incorrectly, perpetuated, and eventually accepted. This ultimately resulted in an acceptance of the errors.

Jane Ann: [shouts] Minchude, Minchude.... O Gad, ah gal go run up meh blood pressure. Minchude, Minchude!

Tan Tan: Who da e bal Minchude this urly marning? Jane Ann ah you? Good marning.

Minchude: Tanty look meh ya.

Jane Ann: Minchude yo tek up ah clothes off ah line aready?

Minchude: Tanty me ain come yah to wok out me sole case enna.

Jane Ann: O Gad Minchude, every marnin so? Eh?

Minchude: Tanty me nah e go no way. Help my God Tanty, ah wayry yo see me yah.

Jane Ann: Way Denton dey?

Minchude: Yo ain calling him to grine ah carn fo mek ah carn pap?

Jane Ann: Gal me have ah win in me stomach and ah wayry talk to Denton.

Minchude: He day-e walk up an down like he dotish. He better go look for wok to do.

The above, a typical conversation, was the dialect of Union Island some fifty years ago, but it has changed in recent years. Here is the interpretation

An early morning in a garden, Jane Ann, an old lady, observed that her niece Minchude who is spending some time with her is nowhere to be found. She calls Minchude loudly but gets no respond. She thinks that Minchude is hearing her but refuses to answer. She also believes that her niece is causing her stress, and that it will eventually cause her to have high blood pressure. She calls Minchude a couple more times.

Tan-Tan, the neighbor hears the bellowing and asks who is calling Minchude so loudly in the morning. She acknowledges Jane Ann and bids her good morning. Minchude finally shows up and says to her aunt, "Aunty I am here." Jane Ann then asks her if she has already taken up the clothes that were hanging on the line. Minchude retorted, "Aunty, I did not come here to work like a slave." Aunty Jane Ann responds to Minchude by asking her if every morning she always has something negative to say to her. Minchude replies, "I swear that I am not doing anything. I am very tired." "Where is Denton?" Jane Ann asks. Minchude responds, "Are you not calling him to grind the corn to make corn porridge?" Jane Ann replies "Girl, I am feeling sick. I have got gas in my stomach. And furthermore, I am tired of asking Denton to do me any favors." Minchude replies by saying that Denton is walking aimlessly as though he is stupid. She further implied that he should find a job.

Although the original dialect has evolved over the years, its influence is still evident throughout the island. There are also some residual effects of the dialect that is present among the younger generation of today. Below are a few phrases that were used then. The italicized captions indicate what they actually mean in today's English. This transcription is meant to conjure up memories from events of the formative years on the island. Enjoy.

1.   Leh-ah-we go ------------------------------------Let us go.

2.   Ah gal deh-deh ----------------------------The girl is there.

3.   Gwan   ---Go on.

4.   She Ugly eh? ---------------------------------Isn't she ugly?

5.   Weh yo sey? ----------------------------What did you say?

6.   Who dah?   ------------------------------------Who is it?

7.   Wah do yo?   ----------------------What happened to you?

8.   Weh yo deh? ------------------------------Where are you?

9.   Wadda e?   -------------What happened/what is wrong?

10. De gal downcay-------------------------The girl is careless.

11. Who-fah chile?--------------------------Whose child is it?

12. Les e naise   ------------------------Be quiet/stop talking.

13. Deh pan yo-----The decision is on you/the onus is on you.

14. Put up yo discose---------No one wants to hear, so please
     don't talk on that subject anymore (discose = discourse).

15. Uha nah e-go no way, nat te-nite-----I am not going
     anywhere, especially tonight.

16. O Gad, nah bring am yah gee ah we, ah gal too caccaba--
     O my God, please do not bring that girl home to us; she is
     utterly useless.

17. Ah tell yo nat to go pan ah plum tree, but o Gad like yo
     break stick in yo A's ----------------------I told you not to
     go on the plum tree, but O my God, you refused to listen.

18. Ah see she dearder day----------- I saw her the other day.

19. Al ah- we ah one-------------- We all are related (family).

20. Me ain goin down deh ennah--------------You know that I
     am not going down there.

21. She deh wid one ah Garfield boy-------She has an
     intimate relationship with one of Mr. Garfield's sons.

52

22. Minchude, war-mek yo en come to school dis marnin? *Minchude, why didn't you come to school this morning?*

23. Doan ley-too by the well yo noh-----*Do not delay at the well, OK?*

24. Uha nah e go no way wid ah gal, she too damn wotlis----*I am not going anywhere with that girl because she is too damn worthless.*

25. Ah warning yo eh-no, ah tell yo to le them strode alone; yo know dey ain't too righted aready -------*Take my advice and leave the Stewarts alone; you already know that they are not mentally sound.*

26. "Ricky en reach home yet? He want ah cut-ass--------- *Ricky is not home yet? He needs a whipping.*

27. Is not Brian alone, Freddy deh-deh too---------*Brian is not there alone; Freddy is there also.*

28. Doh gee Sarah the clothes to wash because she dos do ting to vike-ah-vike---------------------*Do not give Sarah the clothes to wash because she does things carelessly.*

29. Grafton, ah callin yo so long, weh yo deh?-------- *Grafton, I have been calling you for a long time; where are you?*

30. Ah Kashie chook meh pan meh battam foot-------*A thorn has pricked the sole of my foot.*

31. Don't walk on de dotty------------*Do not walk on the dirt.*

32. De bull jumped the cattle------------*The cohabitation of the male and female cattle.*

33. De pig drop dis marnin, it mek nine.-----*The pig gave birth to nine piglets this morning.*

34. De cattle run-meh--------------------------*The cow was running away from me, and I could not keep up with it.*

35. Yo didn know Ce Margin gran daughter have three Pickney? Sid down deh----------------*Did you not know that Ce Morgan's granddaughter has three children? Well, you are not up to date with what's happening.*

36. I don ny'am the lil drop ah vittle yo gee meh--------*I have already eaten the small amount of food that you gave to me.*

37. Next year go mek three years now since McKay John and Goldstan nah-e pull------------------*Next year will be three years since McKay John and Goldstan are enemies.*

38. Leh me gee yo ah la-lick-----*Let me give you a lash at departure (not a whipping). (La-lick was actually a last lick or final lash of gesture when children departed from school to their respective homes).*

39. Way de hell e nack me fah, e shit Pickney fee nack?--*Why did you hit me, did you make a child so that you can hit them?*

40. Gal you get it oh-toe-toe----------------*Girl you have gotten it in abundance.*

41. Marva like too much ah damn commess, ley she go she way---------------------- *Marva is too contentious; do not pay her any attention.*

42. Help my God, if yo ain go and get ah bucket ah water, yo ain gettin a drap ah tea here this marning----------*I swear if you don't fetch a bucket of water, you will not have breakfast this morning.*

43. Weh e call mey fah, weh e want? ---------*What are you calling me for? What do you want?*

44. Yo nah e-nack ah-we like how yo e nack Clouden ennah--- *We are not going to allow you to beat us as you beat Clouden, you know.*

45. Ah tell yo to make de broth; you tellin me Guinea hen bring ram goat---------------------*I told you to make a broth; you are telling me about something unrelated.*

46. Eh noh-o gee me that, cah me too old?----------*Why won't you give that to me, is it because I am too old and not appealing? (Sexual connotation from a female).*

47. Ah hear Ba Mindo tek-in--I heard that Ba Mindo is very ill.

Only fifty years ago, these and many more colloquial phrases were prevalent in Union Island. To get a firsthand experience of these superstitions, one must be in the presence of two or three elders; it will be an event to savor.

From the impetus that led to the writing of Union Island Then and Now, the author made mention of one of the folklore that were prevalent on the island during the twentieth century. It is imperative to share the beliefs and customs of the ancestors because residual effects are still widespread throughout the Caribbean.

a. Do not put your hands on your head because that can hasten the death of your mother.

b. Always put a piece of red thread on the forehead of a baby because it keeps away evil spirits and prevents the child from becoming sick.

c. Never go to bed thirsty because your spirit will come out of you to get water while you sleep.

d. Do not let your babies look at a mirror when they are under one year old. The mirror is considered another world, and if they look at this other world, a spirit can enter their bodies.

e.   Do not sweep at night or open an umbrella indoors because these things can bring you bad luck.

f.   Do not sweep on someone's feet or they may never get married.

g.   Whenever you are sick, you must wipe a wet egg on your face and immediately place it under your bed. This will hasten your recovery.

Then come the local idioms, which are exclusive to Union Island and Union Island alone. At worst, they can conjure up a tremendous amount of laughter.

- *When man dead.......Grass Grow.* This means, whenever the patriarch or father dies, the home is often neglected; this can result in the abandonment of certain rules and principles.

- *Take yo yam and give me ma bag.* This means, I have done everything (job) that you require of me, therefore I need payment right now.

MAROON FESTIVAL

Maroon in the Caribbean today is a festive event. In some countries it has become a huge tourist attraction. Let us now take a look at its original meaning, how it came about, and what it meant to the people of Union Island.

"The Maroon" literally means a runaway slave—referring to slaves who were opposed to oppression and hence fled into the rugged interior of the forest and hills rather than remaining in captivity. It is the same struggle that the black Cimarrones of the Colombian Caribbean Coast faced. After all, there were no alternatives for the slaves; they were mere chattel whose lives were doomed at the hands of their slave masters. Their only place of refuge was the dense forests, which, in most cases led to the highlands. Yet this was a fortress that was precarious. Life was very difficult for these people who had to start life anew under grossly inhospitable conditions—inclement weather in these highlands, white attackers, poisonous snakes, predatory animals, and the inability to obtain and grow food undisturbed. These were just a few of the challenges that they had to endure. Yet even under these adverse conditions, life was better than the sheer brutality, misuse, and abuse at the hands of these evil "Massas" who rendered no form of recompense.

It is reputed that the treatment of African slaves on British sugar colonies was inhumane. The regular form of punishment for eating sugarcane on the plantation, stealing, or even being absent from the plantation for work was being beaten with a stick (even to the point of breaking bones), having to wear a chain around the neck and ankle, and sometimes being incarcerated in a dungeon. There were also more barbaric acts, such as the breaking of limbs, castration, and even beating out of the eyes. Slavery produces cruelty and oppression rather than morality, decency, sympathy, and religion.

There was nothing worthwhile about this wicked institution, and the only way out was to escape. Quite a few slaves made that decision at the expense of their lives. Slave codes indicated that runaways who refused to be arrested might be lawfully killed. Slaves were forbidden to carry arms or to go off their masters' plantations without a written pass, to lift a hand against their masters (even in self-defense), to beat drums, and to hold religious services without a white person present. In addition, it was illegal for slaves to read or write, to gather in groups of more than five, to own property, and to marry. Nevertheless, some slaves still found the courage to escape.

As small as Union Island may be, the slaves of that day were not exempted from the sheer brutality and abuse of this gruesome yet lucrative institution. Remember the story my great grandmother, the late Isabella Roache, told me? "A field-slave on a cotton plantation of Union Island was unable to work because he was sick. That made the slave master furious, and he immediately ordered that he be buried in his current state of uselessness. 'Massa me nah dead yet,' (Master, I am not dead yet), the middle-aged slave pleaded hopelessly for his life, but the slave master retorted angrily, "Carry him and bury him. "The slaves interpreted in their dialect "Carry um go bury um."

It is regrettable that a slave who may have been severely ill succumbed to an untimely grave in that he was forcefully buried alive without remorse. The location of his atrocious burial site is under a huge Hog Plum tree at Bajan Corner on Clifton Road. Bajan Corner attained its name from an old woman named Jestina Noel who was living in that area; she was nicknamed Ce Bajan.

Because of this incident and the location of this atrocious burial, Bajan Corner was always considered haunted by many residents. Many years ago, residents feared walking alone at Bajan Corner during the late hours of night.

Ta Muggy also made mention of another slave whose suffering was less significant. This slave, she said, had his own small shack or living quarters on the cotton plantation. He did not show up for work for two consecutive days. The third day, with no questions asked, the grass roof of his meager dwelling was viciously yanked off to send a message to other slaves. Looking back carefully, we can conclude that such occurrences would have been during the early years of 1901-1909. There was no significant difference between a slave and a so-called free Negro, for the atmosphere of Massa-slave relationship had not truly changed. Unfortunately black people (Africans) in Union Island remained almost as chattel for many years.

Slaves were not permitted to build proper living quarters—not because they did not have the means to do so, but because it was totally forbidden. The man whose roof was yanked off his shack was located where Ms. Eldine Clouden of Clifton now lives. (The current location is adjacent to one of Mr. E. Richards estate). This misdeed was one of the less destructive attacks on a chattel, a rare exception to the rule of that day. Sickness on the plantation was something that was not dealt with favorably; only the fit and healthy were needed. Hence, a slave who was unable to work was nothing but a liability.

Over a period of time, these runaway slaves, the Maroons, banded together to form communities once the strains of life had eventually been alleviated. It was their natural propensity for a communal lifestyle that enabled them to be recognized as a people, officially called the Maroons. Maroons were present on Suriname, Jamaica, Haiti, St. Vincent, Grenada, Dominica, and Cuba. To date, there is no documented history available of slaves in Union Island or Carriacou fleeing their respective plantations for the hills, but the original purpose of this celebration was freedom. The bulk of slaves who came from Africa were primarily from the west coast of Ghana, Cameroon, Nigeria, Senegal, Sierra Leone, Liberia, and Guinea, and they brought their cultures along with them. The customs of the many tribes—The Yoruba, Ashanti, Kisii, Makoa, Adjas, and Fons—were exhibited once per year on Union Island in a cultural union called the Maroon, and later, Maroon Festival.

Up until the 1970s, older folks would speak candidly about the three major tribes that existed in Union Island—the Kisii, Makoa, and Kanka tribes. Each tribe possessed certain salient characteristics; thus, they were easily distinguished one from another. One characteristic of the Makoa tribe is that they are rather reclusive and secretive. The Kisii tribe is said to have originated in Sierra Leone, Liberia, and Guinea, and members were said to have an intrinsic propensity for agriculture.

Let us now return to the Maroon festival of the nineteenth century and the first quarter of the twentieth century. The Maroon festival of Union Island and her sister isle Carriacou happened once a year after the island's harvest. Early that morning, everyone would gather at a designated area in the hills.

An abundance of raw foods was taken to the site to be cooked. With huge pots meticulously placed on three-stoned fires, the people would prepare some of the tastiest dishes in the land. In retrospect, it was a competitive spirit that every cook exhibited on that special day. When cooking was finished and the food was ready, it was blessed. Everyone would eat heartily as they complimented each other on their fine dishes. "Aunt Caroline, ah victual with the rice and peas and jackfish eat good eh?" Then someone in the crowd may answer, "If you want to taste ah good wangoo pwah, step over here and have a mouthful ah mine." "Aunt Jane Ann that is some nice jack fish you have there, gaul," another person might whisper. Amazingly, with many of the older folks, the African dialect was very pronounced, and they spoke very little English.

Everyone was totally immersed in the festivity, and they all had a good time.

Today in the neighboring cay of Carriacou, the annual Maroon festival is much larger than that of Union and is celebrated during the final week of April. It is surely a cultural site to experience. The African attire is no different from that of the Afrocolombianos; the early African slaves of Colombia. It will be fascinating for first-time visitors to experience such festive atmosphere.

Cultural colors are evident in the African attire.

Unlike Union Island where the African culture has dwindled significantly, the sound of the African drum and accompanying folk dances are still a force to be reckoned with in the sister island of Carriacou.

As mentioned earlier, the original Maroon festival was held annually on the hillsides or in the bushes; it was a huge event that lasted all day. During the later years, Clifton Hill became the principal spot for this festivity.   This festivity involves the entire population.   Foodstuffs consisting mainly of meats, fish, rice, flour, cornmeal, peas, beans, ground provisions, and fruits were brought to the locations to be cooked. Some of the largest cooking pots were brought on site and were placed on a three-stoned fire. Firewood was the only energy used to fuel the fire, for that was the custom of the natives even at home prior to the use of the gas and electrical stoves. Some homes still practice this tradition today.

Cooking, however, was preceded by a libation—the pouring of rum, wine, or water on the ground as an offering to the ancestors. There was plenty of food for everyone. Curry goat, Pigeon peas and rice, fry Jack Fish, Conch, sand potatoes, Wangoo and okras, stew chicken, Green-corn dumplings, Pelau, and Wangoo Pwah were available all day long. Everyone ate bountifully; no one was a stranger on that day. The Maroon's prime purpose, coupled with the libation, was to give homage to the gods and ancestors and to ask for their blessings on the future. Yes, this was the crux of this mass gathering. And so a huge portion of the food was taken to the local cemetery, where it was put into huge banana leaves and placed on the tombstones of the deceased. Some of this food was also tossed into the sea, for water represented life.

The African cultural dance that was performed after the cooking and dining is still prevalent on Union Island after a forceful divorce from the motherland some 350 years ago. These cultural dances were done to the beat of the African drums, and out of these remarkable sounds came an intrinsic yearning that commanded the body of an onlooker to respond involuntarily.

Open La-La ah me way dey, open la-la down dey
Open La-La ah me way dey, open la-la down dey

Open la-La ah dah way day, open la-La down dey

Open la-La ah dah way day, open la-La down dey

The crowd would sings; the sound of the African dialect became flagrant as the African drum rolled simultaneously with conviction.

The matriarch takes command of the floor, dressed in long African attire, accompanied by two or three men attired in less conspicuous colors. Heads wrapped with a matching fabric, the women would dance in unison as the rolls of the African drum intensified. The tempo suddenly decreases, but would pick up momentum again, enticing these women to dance with more vigor. Then instantaneously, one or two of the women would wave their wide skirts over the head of a drummer and dance as the crowd erupted with new energy.

These dancers danced gracefully with passion until it was time for another song. One female would again sensually dance her way to the lead drummer and entice him to stop by placing her hands on his drum. The other drummers, immediately aware of her sensuous appeal, would instantly stop their drumming. She was in total command, dictating what she wanted, how she wanted it, and when she wanted it. Then almost immediately, the drum would roll again as another song was sung:

Too late, too laa-late, too late too laa-late,
Too late, too laa-late wee mamma bell shango.
Dem gal laden, dem gal laden, dem gal laden
Leh ah-wee go ah labay
Dem gal may-may, dem gal may-may
Dem gal may-may lay ah we go ah Trespass.
Hezekiah don't care, Hezekiah don't care,
Hezekiah don't care he love he Theo...Dora.

The transition from one song to another was carried out through the duration of the festival.

Ty runaway, Ty runaway,
Ty runaway, Ty ran away O.
You nar have mamma, you nar have papa a,
Ty ran away
Ty runaway, Ty runaway ah Batica
Yo nar have mamma, yo nar have papa a
Ty ran away.

These women controlled the streets where the Maroon activities were held with nonstop action. The incessant singing of African folk songs, drumming, and dancing continued with songs such as "Clear the way, clear the way O," and "I, I, I sally-boo lay, I boo lay- lay I sally-boo lay" into the late afternoon or night to end the Maroon celebration. Fortuitously, after each Maroon Festival, the nights were never void of an intermittent shower or, at best, a copious rainfall.

A typical Maroon night in Carriacou; resembles that of yesterday's Maroon of Union Island.

THE AMERINDIANS

Let us expand our horizons by taking a look at the Amerindians -another race of people who walked the soil of Union Island thousands of years before Christopher Columbus (sighting), Antoine Regaud, Jean Augier, Samuel Spann, Charles Mulzac, and Mr. E. Richards. They were the first settlers of Union Island -people who were never weary of a community lifestyle.

Like many communities, they toiled the land and planted many root crops. Their principal food source derived from the sea, for fishing was an integral part of their livelihood. They also fed extensively on the turtles that are native to the region. Manicoo and iguanas were also hunted for food.

Archeologists claimed that these people were in existence in these regions some fifty-four hundred years BC. The presence of numerous artifacts on Union island is indicative of a community that once existed and flourished there. Unfortunately, there is no documented history of these people, so they can only be honored by virtue of their tangible past -their artifacts. But where are these artifacts now?

For decades, adventurous visitors dug up pots and many other valuable utensils throughout the island. During such time, no authority from St. Vincent & the Grenadines assumed guardianship of what was being excavated. Sadly the bountiful treasures that were unearthed never made their way to any museum of St. Vincent and the Grenadines but instead were swindled and taken away to different soils. The question that many Unionites have been asking themselves in recent years is this: "Are we not deserving of the island's natural heritage and artifacts?" Firstly, these Amerindians were annihilated and then the artifacts that they left behind were stolen. As a result, the history of the Amerindians of Union Island sometime around 5400 BC and onward is now etched into the wilderness of nothingness.

Some residents who were goaded to unearth these

treasures have attested to what they have seen and found. Artifacts unearthed at the beaches of Union Island included stone tools, bowls, smoking vessel, shards, pottery, jewelry, amulets, clay pots, arrowheads, and Ica stones. The late Mr. Clem Stewart, the third generation of the renowned McDowell Stewart, speaks vehemently of his encounter with a group of foreigners who were trespassing on his land at Chatham Bay. "They had with them instruments to detect objects that were buried," he said. "I chased them out," he continued, "They never asked for permission to come on my land; they came to steal all the gold." But Mr. Clem Stewart was not always present at Chatham, so time and time again he encountered large areas on his property that had been dug up. The roots of huge Manchineel trees were left exposed or partially covered. It is reputed that some artifacts that were unearthed from the numerous harbors of Union Island can be found at the museum on the neighboring island of Carriacou.

BOAT LAUNCHING

The subject of vessels is important here for it is an integral part of the lives of Unionites. But before we can delve into the meat of this matter, it is quantum sufficit that we take a look at one of the most celebrated events in Union Island during its heyday. Launching!

Although Frigate Rock may have been a feasible spot for building vessels, Top Yonder Bay was the principal shipyard for most boat builders of Union Island, period. The early years of the twentieth century give rise to the building of the Paragon, Priscilla, Pursuer, and Providence up until July 1974 when the last boat, Unity, was built and launched. Let us take a look at one of our cultural practices that died almost four decades ago.

When a huge boat or vessel is completed, the logical thing that follows is the launching. Because of the tedious nature of this undertaking, the owner makes it his greatest endeavor to see that everything is meticulously put into place to facilitate a smooth process.

The boat/vessel-launching day is an entire day's activity wrapped up in festivity. The entire island descends on Top Yonder Bay to perform the traditional ceremony related to launching in Union Island. Like a newborn child, the prospective boat or vessel is assigned a godmother and godfather. The owner, priest, or minister, along with other important personnel, proceeds to bless the craft. Praying and singing of hymns are done on site, followed by a libation that is performed at the stern of the craft. The libation is the sprinkling and pouring of rum and/or water on the craft, asking for the guidance and protection of God and the ancestors whenever the boat makes a voyage at sea.

A female then places a cake on her head, hands on her hips, and dances to the beat of the African drum or other instruments—a spectacle indeed! A collection bucket is made available for anyone who can make a financial contribution. After the dance, the cake is cut into many slices and distributed on the spot.

As in a home in Union Island that has just lost a loved one, foodstuff, liquors, gifts, money, and livestock are showered in abundance at the home of the vessel owner ahead of time. The cooking part of this ceremony is the women's responsibility, and they are the absolute best in the region. Elaborate cooking is done to feed the entire village of participants and onlookers who assemble at the launching site. The food is taken to the site when the craft is to be shoved and pulled into the water by every man, woman, and child. The entire launching process is fully accomplished by the cooperative efforts of the mass gathering at Top Yonder Bay. It is phenomenal for a first-timer to observe the entire process from when the craft leaves the location where it was built until it reaches its final destination, the sea, where it remains afloat.

It is traditional for boats and vessels of Union Island to bear the name of the wife or daughter of the owner. A typical example is the Vessel Sylvia E. M. of the '70s that was owned by three Unionites: Paul, Peter, and Mano. Sylvia is the wife of Mr. Paul Wilson. The E stands for Elizabeth, the wife of the late Peter Wilson, and the M stands for Mary, the wife of Mano Hutchinson. The latter two are now deceased.

The flag, which bears the name of the boat, is tightly wrapped and placed on the deck of boat. The large gathering is eager and impatient to find out the name given to this new vessel. All eyes are fixed on the owner, who stands way above on the deck, ready to announce the name of this virgin craft. The eventual announcement is met with joyful pandemonium by the fleet of onlookers. The blowing of conch shell, the cheering, and the beat of the African drum bring more awakening to the already lively morning.

The vessel must now be placed in a ready position before the entire process of launching can be performed. The vessel is kept upright, with many long poles attached to its side and wedged firmly into the earth. Each pole is numbered, and a male with a sharp axe is assigned to each pole. There he stands alert, awaiting his instruction to chop without floundering; this can be a tense moment for each assignee. With myriad instructions being shouted in this ruckus-like atmosphere, the enthusiasm of onlookers grows with clapping, cheering, and hollering. The chopping of the pole is meticulously done; to falter can render some damage to the craft. The point of culmination arises when the last pole that carries the enormous weight of the craft is chopped, turning the craft on its side and in a ready position for the launching.

A long rope is extended way into the sea to an anchor, which is placed exactly in the vicinity where the boat should be able to float without its keel touching the floor of the sea. This anchor should be sturdy enough to endure the strenuous task of the pulling. A line of people is tethered to the other end of the rope, with a block and tackle placed midway to ease the process of launching (pull the craft into the sea). Under the keel of the craft are tree trunks or logs lined up as rollers to aid its smooth transition into the water. These rollers are placed slightly ahead of the craft, to the spot where it is supposed to move. The stern of the boat is also secured with ropes to prevent it from leaning and sliding out of control and incurring injuries. With instruction, men, women, and children grab the rope firmly and begin pulling, but in the opposite direction of the boat; others literally shove the boat in the direction of the sea.

The pulling and shoving continues, with lulls after each effort so that participants can rest during such a tiresome task. When the vessel reaches the water, a loud cacophony erupts as everyone is jubilated. The atmosphere becomes a gala as the crew is energized to push the boat further into the water. As soon as the vessel begins to float, a few bottles of liquor are smashed onto its stern. This symbolizes a task well done.

Ashore, the bacchanal climaxes with elaborate eating, drinking, socializing, and dancing to the beat of the African drum and other instruments brought for that special event. This entire day's activity continues until sundown, and everyone happily goes home. Later in the street, the feeling of community is still evident as residents can be found fondly discussing the success of the day's event.

Sadly, this major event is approximately four decades removed from the soil of Union Island. We can only crave its renaissance.

FISHING

The absence of a viable fishing industry represents a significant loss of Union Island's livelihood and culture. The island is now experiencing a drastic reduction in fishing-related activities along the once-trafficked shorelines. As a result, it now appears that the last sound of the conch shell has gracefully made its way into total oblivion. Well almost. Esteem names such as Aaron Douglas, Woodley Cox, Sylvan Hutchinson, David John (Gayman), Willy Daniel (Santas), Ozias Paul, and Gifted Wilson were the vertebral column of the fishing industry that existed in Union Island for a long period of time. These names were household names to every resident who lived on Union Island during the '60s, '70s, and '80s. After all, the island is small enough that everyone knows each other.

Is there really a shortage of fish in Union Island? Just two decades ago, such a notion could not have been conceived. But time has changed drastically. Residents of Union Island are now living in a time when old ideas are superseded by new ideas. Somewhat. Can Unionites realistically believe that they can erect a protective covering over their culture that will safely shield it from extinction without employing adequate maintenance? This is contingent on evolution and evolution alone.

There is a complete shortage of home cooking along the local fishing grounds. So where does subsistence comes in? Subsistence always meant a lot to Union Island and the rest of the Grenadines. For the record, a subsistent economy is an economy in which enough food is grown, hunted, or gathered to provide for the people. A surplus is grown only if a community desires or needs to trade with neighboring communities. But to the dismay of many, even subsistent fishing has dwindled to an unprecedented low. Of course it is unrealistic to expect things to remain one way forever, but isn't it baffling that it is now status quo to be buying fish regularly from the neighboring islands? Of course, there must be a feeling of guilt and inadequacy. After all, Ashton Bay, Basin, and Chatham Bays were large breeding grounds for jack fish that once made up a major part of the gross domestic product of our island. And Jack fish in particular were once prevalent in their diets. This begs the question: Why haven't the wangoo and okra been mentioned as Union Island's national dish?

Remember long ago when the aforementioned fishermen cast their large nets at Campbell and made huge catches? Remember when many fathers and young men would descend on the shores to meet these same fishermen and to help haul the catch ashore? Remember when these fishermen, after spending numerous hours at sea, would return with their catch to be greeted by an elder, in turn giving a small portion of their catch to such elders?

Remember when the sound of the conch shell was the means to alert the community that fish was available and being sold? Are the baby boomers the final bearers of these memories in that when they die, the priceless memories will as well? Oh well.

These fishermen were rather determined and purposeful with the little that they started out with. Their fishing techniques increased over the years out of necessity and through an increase of knowledge, awareness, skills, and determination. After all, they were the patriarchs and were responsible for providing food, clothes, and shelter for their families. These were some of the cogent values and customs that were etched into the culture, and they had known it no other way.

Out of big catches, boatloads of Jack fish, was transported to Grenada on a regular basis for sale; the island of Grenada was the sole market for these huge catches. When the fishermen could not sell all of these Jack fish, they would barter for ground provision, mangoes, and other fruits. The village was happy to meet and greet the fishermen at the shores when they would return to Union Island. The same boats that left laden with fish a couple of days earlier would return laden with mangoes, fruits, and other ground provisions. Remember when these fishermen would freely give some of their mangoes to the children standing watchfully? Today the island's fishermen have abandoned the use of seines and trammels. Unfortunately the art of fishing, or the legacy of fishing at this scale, has come to an end.

Were there no fruits of youth industry planted in the hearts and minds of the younger generation? The author mentioned earlier that many baby boomers and subsequent generations have immigrated unwittingly to other countries in search of a better life; that, of course, has become a trend in itself. Nevertheless, the question must still be posed: Where are the knowledge, beliefs, morals, laws, arts, and customs of Union Island's society? The values? It is high time to know these things; many are convinced that the virtues and backbone of the culture is nearly lost. Which do you like better, Union Island then, or now?

TURTLES IN THE REGION

The coral-filled waters of the Grenadines have been home to the Hawksbill, Leatherback, Loggerhead, and Green turtles for centuries. Residents know very well that the beaches of Big Sand, Basin, Point Lookout, Ms. Irene, Ms. Pay, Chatham, Bloody Bay, and Queensbury Point have been safe havens for these reptilian wonders that come in annually to proliferate. Today, surprisingly, the Loggerhead is not as frequently seen on the sand during their gestation period as they were in the past.

Regional fishermen seldom see the Loggerhead even at sea. It is said that this specie of turtle are endangered internationally. During the month of March—the gestation period—these reptiles approach their place of birth three times in forty-five days, eager to bury their fortune under the densely fine fossils. There these secured embryos take approximately two months to hatch. To poachers, the demand for this seasonal commodity is insatiable; this turtle is considered a delicacy when boiled. Long ago, poachers were adept at identifying the fresh tracks made by these sea creatures whenever they came upon land to lay their eggs. Some of them were clever enough to determine the age of the turtle by carefully observing the texture of the freshly laid eggs. They could also determine whether it was the first time that a turtle had returned to the place of its birth to lay eggs.

But turtle hunting is not novel in the waters of the Grenadines. It has been a legacy that dated back many, many years ago. In fact, the French used turtles as a source of food during the 1760's when they first laid foot on Union Island. The shell of this reptile was also a valuable commodity for trade. But even before the existence of the French, the Amerindians used the meat of turtles as the principal source of their diet. Today, although there is a decline in numbers, turtles are still plentiful in the region.

The Grenadines are home to these four species of turtles, which are seen in abundance at the Tobago Cays Resort all year round but are more proliferous during their gestation periods.

The Carib Grackle (black bird) and the iguana are also native to these four pristine islands. This is a spectacle for tourist and visitors.

For a long time, the natives of Union Island have considered the meat and eggs of these reptiles an invaluable commodity compared to the meat of other sea animals. For that reason no one would pass up the opportunity to unearth these delectable eggs and then catch the turtle fifteen days later. Fortunately, the Union Island Environmental Attackers, a nonprofit organization, has become the vanguard in hopes of preventing the extinction of these wonders and the servicing of other meaningful projects. Those other projects range from quarterly island cleanups, which address sanitation and garbage removal, to health talks at schools, adopt-a-tree programs, and a host of valuable issues that are good for the island as a whole.

The Union Island Environmental Attackers patrol numerous beaches to promote the successful nesting of these endangered sea creatures. Because local poachers are the number-one predator, the organization monitors the eggs until the hatchlings are born and head to sea to face yet other predatory challenges. It is estimated that an average of one out of every one thousand Leatherback Turtles, (largest specie) survives to adulthood.

To discourage poachers and inquisitive hands from unearthing these embryos, there is a maximum fine of $5,000. Through seminars, the people must be informed and educated about the plight that these turtles face to keep their population alive when the odds are stacked highly against their survival in the wild. On a turtle watch of March 2011, one of those ageless wonders (Leatherback Turtle) inherited the European name Analese. This successful tagging was conducted by the Union Island Environmental Attackers under the stewardship of Mr. Roseman Adams, an entrepreneur of Clifton. We hope that with other successful tagging in the future, prospective turtles will bear names that are native to these shores—names such as Lydian, Janie, Annie, Sheila, Serena, Norma, Caroline, Virginia, Susana, Leah, and Thelma. The myriad of sentiments that accompany these familiar names surely wouldn't hurt either.

The ecology of the region must be protected, and that encompasses the mangrove coastland and shallow reefs that circumnavigate this skimpy landmass that is equivalent to a mere 3.5 sq. miles.

♦♦♦□*Chapter Four*

THE THINGS WE USED TO DO

The declination of the cotton crop during the late nineteenth century gave way to other means of survival on the island. The Mulzacs were owners of many vessels, and they transported cargo regionally to other Caribbean countries. They fished extensively in the waters of the Grenadines and also had numerous livestock. This legacy is one that was handed down through the years and had become a way of life for the people of Union Island. There were also other means of livelihood that the people practiced. Regrettably, they were struck violently by evolution and have since met their demise. These encompass the corn & pea crops as well as the exportation of tamarind, Cornish, Divi-Divi, crabs, chicken (fowl), sea moss, and sugar apples to Trinidad. Their absence represent a significant economic lost to the island.

There are some practices that once were a dominant part of the culture when subsistence was indeed integral to the lives of the people on this little island. The following are just a few.

Corned Fish

Fish catching has always been fundamental to every fisherman in Union Island, and although there isn't a huge market on the island for the freshly caught product, no one can dispute its mammoth contribution to the diets of every Unionite. Corn fish is the fish that is salted and dried in the sun, a method of preservation used for centuries by the natives. With this method, the fish can be kept for months before use. It is similar to the salted codfish or Bacalao that is used universally.

This is how corn fish is done on Union Island. First the scales are removed from the fish, and then the head is sliced in half, all the way through the dorsal fins to the tail. The fish still remains in one piece as the intestines and gills are removed. Numerous vertical incisions are made in the flesh so that the salt can penetrate rather easily. A dose of salt is meticulously sprinkled into every incision of the fish's flesh. The fish is then folded and placed into a container for at least an hour so that the salt can penetrate further into the flesh. It is then placed in the sun to dry. Long ago, the choice location was the roof of the external kitchen, where two days of drying would extract 90 percent of the water. This dry, salted fish could then be stored in a cool, dry location for months before use.

Though this art of corning fish is still practiced on Union Island, it hasn't been properly bequeathed to the younger generation. As a result, this fine art and skillful method of preservation is not utilized enough throughout the island.

Dried Okra

The okra crop is very important in Union Island and has multiple uses in many dishes, but its primary use is to make kalalloo—a well-known dish that is home to the Caribbean. Due to the perishable nature of the okra crop, its shelf life is no longer than a week, at best. Because of the single rainy season experienced in Union Island, this important crop cannot be available all year round. Therefore, the drying of okra is simply a process of preservation whereby it may be available for use during the severe dry season. A huge quantity of freshly picked okra is sliced into ½-inch rings and placed on a canvas or caucus bag to be dried in the sun. The drying process takes approximately three days, and the okra is subsequently stored in a container to be used at a later date. The combination of corn and okra, both locally grown products, makes up the once cherished and tacitly acknowledged national dish, wangoo and okra.

This is how it is done: The dried product is placed into a large pot, where it is cooked very dry. The content is then placed into a mortar and pestle, where it is thoroughly crushed or pounded fine and subsequently sieved. The sieved content, though brown in color, is very potent when used with ground sesame seeds (locally called benna). This is used as a substitute for freshly picked okra. A tedious task, eh? Yes it is, but that is what was once done with passion when the refrigerator was

was nonexistent. Obviously, this art of preserving Okra is not practiced anymore in Union Island. Instead, other vegetables and fruits are now obtained from St. Vincent, where they are available all year-round.

Local Coffee (wild coffee)

The wild coffee plant—a small, leafy plant that is approximately two feet tall—is grown extensively throughout the island as a wild menacing shrub. The very small seeds, which are almost rock-hard in texture, are extracted from their long, skinny pods. They are baked very dry to remove approximately 90 percent of the liquid. This makes the seeds relatively brittle and very easy to grind. They are then ground fine in a grain mill and packaged in an airtight container and ready to be used as a beverage. It is ground much the same as regular coffee and has a delectable odor commensurate to its fine taste. During the first half of the 20th Century, this product was made at almost every home on the island. This fine, appetizing product, though marketable, was never sold locally or regionally. The roots of the wild coffee plants also have medicinal value. They are scraped, boiled, and used for severe bellyaches and pain. This locally made medicine is very bitter but effective.

Okra Seeds (beverage)

In this case, the okra is left to dry on the okra plant for several weeks. The dry pods are picked, shelled, cleaned, and then placed in the sun for further drying. These tiny assorted okra seeds that are half the size of the pigeon pea are carefully baked dry in a wide pot to a dark brown color. Finally, they are ground in a grain mill—the same mill that is used to grind the pulpy kernels of corn. This fine, powdery product is then placed into an airtight jar to maintain its shelf life. It is reputed that this now archaic coffee-like beverage was considered second to none, especially when mixed with milk. Rumors have it that it was a better-tasting product than the above-mentioned coffee drink. This product, like wild coffee beverage, can also be used as a marketable commodity both locally and regionally.

Farine

Farine, as it is called in most English-speaking countries, is a product that is known throughout the Caribbean and the world. It is made from the roots of the Cassava plant. Its origin is South America, and it is widely used in Brazil. Cassava—or yucca, as most Spanish-speaking countries call it -is said to be the greatest starch-yielding crop in the world. Farine is mentioned here because its once hefty production in Union Island has now dwindled down to zero. The process of manufacture entails removing the skin of the cassava by scraping. The cassava is then washed with water, preferably seawater. This brilliant white product is then grated with a large, locally made grater (metal or tin punched numerous times with a nail) and then squeezed dry of all its liquid. The liquid is collected to use as starch, and the fiber-like product is sieved and patched in a huge copper pot. The end product is farine.

But there are two types of cassava grown in Union Island: the bitter and the sweet. The bitter cassava is poisonous if eaten raw. The deadly component is hydrocyanic acid (HCN). When ingested, it impacts the respiratory process negatively, which results in asphyxiation and ultimately death. The good news is that the deadly component in bitter cassava can be removed by extracting the liquid through squeezing. In that case, the valuable starchy liquid can be collected and used for starching clothes and other uses. Boiling is another means of removing the poisons when there is a need to consume it immediately. There is no need for alarm here; residents dating back to the West Coast of Africa have used this product for centuries. They are quite adept at their craft.

Uttermost attention must be paid to loose animals in the vicinity during this entire farine-making process. If any animals were to drink of the squeezed liquids of the grated cassava, they, too, would surely die. During the 1950s, some residents lost domesticated animals in that manner. When there is a large quantity of cassava to process, this tedious method usually takes the residents an average of three to four days to complete. When the bulk of work has been too much for one day and the grated cassava must remain overnight, the green leaves from the lime tree is placed with the mixture so as to prevent it from fermenting or spoiling. That was the sole means of preservation during those early days.

Making farina was important on Union Island. One principal site of production was at Clifton, in the vicinity of Mrs. Amutel's Supermarket. Residents of Clifton would gather around the almond tree on Clifton Harbor, scraping, grating, and straining to make the farine. Food to feed everyone was cooked on site, with dry wood used to fuel the fire—a common practice among the early inhabitants. That was the true definition of community in Union.

Churning Butter

Making butter in Union Island? Yes that was done too. The milk used for churning butter was milked from cows. A cow won't give up the bulk of its milk unless the calf is allowed to suck first. Now a milking cow can be milked twice during a half-hour period. So the calf is allowed to suck while the cow relinquishes 85 percent of its milk in the first milking. The other 15 percent is collected after a two or three-minute hiatus when the calf begins to suck again. According to older folks, that final milk is richer, so it is from this that a small quantity is taken for the purpose of making butter.

The fresh milk is placed into a wide container such as a soup bowl. The milk is left overnight, and the cream, which settles at the top, is carefully removed and placed into a narrow-necked bottle like a regular wine bottle. The cork is then placed firmly over the bottle and left in a dark area until the next day. This is done everyday until the bottle is almost full; then it is left for another three months before the churning process can begin.When this product is ready to be churned, local sea salt is placed into the bottle to activate the churning process and to aid in the washing procedure. The neck of the bottle is held tightly and is continuously stricken into a soft billow-like material until the content of the bottle is consolidated into a single mass.

The content that now looks light yellow in color is carefully poured into a container where it is cleaned and washed with additional salt and water. The end product is a fresh jar of homemade butter—free of all chemicals and preservatives. Almost every household that reared cattle during the better part of the twentieth century made this fine product, and it lasted as long as they wanted it to. Margarine usage in Union Island is alarmingly high; margarines now more commonly used in Union Island is alarmingly high; margarines now more commonly used than butter. According to a recent newsletter by Dr. David Williams, a renowned physician, the consumption of margarine by humans is much more dangerous than smoking cigarettes. Yet cigarettes smoking is said to be the major causative agent of lung cancers—80 percent, to be exact.

As we can see, the product of the milk's cream, butter, was quite a collective effort. Tedious? Yes! But enjoyable in a time when there was not much to do; it surely was time well spent.

If the question "How is local butter made?" were asked of generations X and Y, they may not know anything relating to this local custom. Alas, this is gone, too; yes, it is a thing of the past.

Guava Jam

At one time, the guava fruit was abundant on Union Island. Children tended to favor it more than any other fruit except plums. Amazingly, this delicious yellow fruit contains more vitamin C than most citrus fruits. There were two species of guava back then. The interior of these two species found in Union Island and the Caribbean were red and white, locally called "red gut" and "white gut," respectively. Almost every home had at least two guava trees, and besides being eaten ripe, this highly aromatic fruit was used to make jam (jelly), cheese, and other confections.

Now this is a curtailed version of how guava jam is made in Union. Selected ripe guavas are placed into a large pot with clean drinkable water. The contents are thoroughly boiled to a pulp and sieved meticulously to remove the numerous seeds. A large amount of sugar is added, along with spices, lemon juice, and other condiments, and the liquid is again boiled so that more that 60 percent of the water evaporates. The lukewarm content is poured into a jar-like bottle and allowed to cool. The resulting numerous bottles of homemade jam is children's delight.

Fire on Top; Fire Below

The author will be remiss if he failed to mention roast bakes in this section. This is bread that is baked in a particular way by the people of Union Island; creativity is the keyword here. Every Unionite utilizes a steel pot for the purpose of baking bread, locally called "bakes. "These bakes are cooked in a huge pot and covered with a flat, circular cover that is a slightly larger than the diameter of the pot. A mild fire is placed on top and also under the pot, giving ample time for the bake to rise slowly and to be baked proportionately without being burned. Get the idea? This is something that Unionites are noted for: "Fire on Top-Fire Below."

Roast bakes and a cup of Santa Maria or Jumbee Bush tea with fresh cow's milk. Yes! We got that a few minutes before we left for school. We got it most mornings, for that matter. We came home after tying-out the sheep, goats, or cattle or after toting water from a nearby well or the public cistern only to be greeted with a couple of hot roast bakes. The butter that was put inside the bake would sometimes melt and run all the way down our elbows. Well, not only can we remember those early days; the fact is we cannot forget them. They are the salient memories that stay with us forever. Did we mention our favorite, the "coconut bakes? "We will stop here and promise not to conjure up any more of these provocative memories. We can only hope that this custom can remain and make its mark as Union Island's breakfast of choice.

But baking was not restricted to pots, as described above; a homemade oven was at every home. I can still imagine the smell of freshly baked bread, sweetbread, cakes, and a variety of pastries coming out of these concrete ovens every Saturday afternoon. The only homes void of this unforgiving aroma were those of the Seventh Day Adventists, whose baking was done primarily on Fridays before sunset. The average size of these ovens was 5'x5'x6'. They were built of Portland cement, sand, and selected stone that was referred to as firestones. These firestones were used because they retained the tremendous heat made by preheating these ovens at high temperatures. Firewood was used to fuel the fires for preheating these ovens prior to placing the bread and pastries inside.

Mr. Hardy Ackie, a resident of Ashton, was one of the typical oven builders of those days, and he knew his craft pretty well. These ovens, which supplanted their predecessors, the clay ovens, were dome-shaped (or like a "U" turned upside down) with a large door. It is reputed that these ovens were ideal for baking, for their retention of heat was enormous. The right side of this oven had an outlet for cleaning the ash after preheating. Unfortunately, these ovens are no more; the modern day oven has supplanted this ancient work of art.

Fires

Long ago, our ancestors kept their fires burning constantly. The presence of a fire burning at one's home was meant to keep out evil spirits and insects. Fires were always burning on a large tree trunk or stump in one's yard somewhere. If for any reason a resident were without fire at her home, she would send a bearer to her neighbor's home to get a fire stick. Because of the community spirit, that good gesture of response was not considered much; it was common, something that was expected.

Tobacco Pipe

Unlike today, when cigarettes are prevalent throughout every community, the pipe was the choice gadget for smoking. Cigarette lighters and matches were not used then; a small fire-stick was used to light the pipes. Older folks (men as well as women) could be seen with this device at the corner of their mouths puffing the freshly dried tobacco. As soon as the sun went down, so did the garden hoe, and then the pipe emerged from a ledge or a hidden corner near a water goblet. It was routine. It's like the televisions that have become an indelible part of our daily lives. A minuscule few would be able to remember those good old days, or golden old day, if you will. As happened with many other customs that preceded this current generation and vanished, the pipe is almost obsolete on Union Island. And mind you, there are no records of lung cancer among the ancestors. How fortunate.

The Unionite

The year 1975 marked the birth of Union Island's first newspaper. The founder, Mrs. Cleo Scrubb-Kirby, was a Unionite by birth and had just returned home after spending numerous years abroad. This remarkable paper she named the Unionite, was a sign of patriotism that she was proud to exhibit. She was both the editor and publisher of this tabloid, which the residents saw once each month. Every month when the paper was published, many excited citizens made door-to-door visits to every nook and cranny of the island to ensure that the paper was published, many excited citizens made door-to-door visits to every nook and cranny of the island to ensure that the paper was sold. To date, it is the first paper to have been manufactured and sold on the island.

This newspaper kept the natives apprised of all local activities and occurrences and also featured community development in the rest of the Grenadine Islands. In the Unionite, Cleo stated that the intention of the newly founded paper was to help Unionites at home and abroad stay in touch. It also offered news on historical and current events by promoting community development while featuring people who had helped to develop the island in the past. She went on to say that the paper offered an outlet for local expression and cultural creativity and that she hoped that Unionites, wherever they were, would get the message. All the writers were residents of Union Island, and the paper encouraged short stories and other contributions from neighboring islanders as well as other countries. Each edition featured outstanding personalities in the community.

In one of the editions of 1975, The Unionite featured the centennial anniversary of the St. Matthias Anglican Church, celebrated on Sunday, May 11, 1975. The paper also featured the late Mr. Tyrell Harvey, his venture abroad, and the first means of transportation, which he made available to his people.

Unfortunately, this vibrant young woman (Cleo) left Union Island a few years later to reside abroad. Regrettably, this led to the imminent death of the Unionite-the paper never resurfaced. It is reputed that this vivacious woman (Cleo) died in 2008 at her home in the UK.

Another newspaper that attained notoriety during its brief tenure on the island was the **Daylight**. Lennox "Bomba" Charles, a Unionite who is currently living abroad, introduced this paper a few months after the final publication of the Unionite. Unfortunately, this paper lasted little more than one year.

The people of Union Island are thankful to Mrs. Cleo Scrub-Kirby and Lennox Charles for their valued contributions.

HERBAL REMEDIES

An ancient philosopher stated, "It is it better to know the patient who has the disease than to know the disease that the patient has." Really?

Well, it is safe to state emphatically that the tradition of folk medicine has played an indispensable role on Union Island for centuries. Some medicines may have been invented out of desperate search for relief from ailments that plagued their communities. We are also aware that they brought some of the herbal traditions with them during the Transatlantic Slave Trade. Plants, the only source of all medicines of that time, were abundant in every nook and cranny of the island. The unfortunate truth is that the uses of herbal medicine on the island have been in serious decline since conventional medicines have gained footing in this society. Medical pharmacology is a rapidly expanding field of study because new drugs are being developed nearly every day? Most drugs in use today come from three natural sources and plants are the principals of these three?

Once upon a time, a long, long time ago on Union Island, the kitchen was the hospital, clinic, or medical center. That was where grandmothers and mothers would quickly concoct a remedy for many ailments. The Seed-Under-Leaf plant was for cold and fever. The mint bush was used for gas removal and settling of the bowel. Many of the locally grown herbs have healed the sick, cleansed the leper, recovered sight for the blind, and of course, set at liberty those that are bruised—just to take a draft from the Bible.

Aloe Vera, known by the Egyptians as the plant of immortality some 6000 years ago, is a native plant of Africa that does very well in St. Vincent and the Grenadines. It is reputed that Aristotle (the father of medicine) asked Alexander the Great to conquer the island of Socotra so that his army would have access to the abundant fields of aloe. This plant is a member of the lily family; the juice or gel from the leaves contains powerful healing compounds. It is widely used to treat minor skin irritations, wounds, and hair loss. One of the best stomach cleansers in the entire herb kingdom, it is well known for its ability to eliminate common gastrointestinal problems and shows promise in treating type 2 diabetes. Its value both orally and topically is unbelievable; this plant has been used for centuries and has remarkable healing properties. The obnoxious taste, mind you, may be daunting to even the hardened users of this plant, but its remarkable value supersedes all deterrents. The cliché "no pain no gain" applies in this instance; anything worth achieving will be difficult. Many users attest to the powerful rejuvenating properties that stimulate the body's own repair mechanisms and aid most health problems. Aloe taken first thing in the morning does the body wonders. The fleshy part of the plant can be blended with fresh orange or pineapple juice and other favorable condiments, improving the taste.

Topically it does a magnificent job in healing the skin of burns, scars, shingles, warts, acne, and even wrinkles from aging. Internally, aloe is said to help cancer patients. For sufferers of lung cancer, it is said that the continuous use of aloe activates the white blood cells and promotes growth of noncancerous cells. Aloe is highly alkaline, and in medical science it is well known that cancerous cells cannot survive in an alkaline environment. Aloe is also good for patients afflicted with the following: asthma, epilepsy, arthritis, rheumatism, heartburn, diabetics, liver and kidney problems, intestinal worms, prostate problems, urinary tract infection. The rhyme, or Aloins, in medical terms, has been used as a local laxative for many, many years ago. To many, it is considered an irritant laxative; it may have adverse effects if consumed irresponsibly. But like any over-the-counter or innocuous drugs, prescription is absolutely necessary. All herbs, if taken in excess, can impact the body negatively. Therefore, one must be particularly moderate and discrete in consumption of Aloins. These excellent detoxifiers have been grossly under-used by the people in the Caribbean.
Here are many of the local herbs with significant medicinal value. These were the only solution in a time when doctors and medical facilities were not in place many years ago:

1. **Hypertension (high blood pressure):** Hour grass, trumpet bush, Aloe Vera, Celery, and carailli

2. Diabetes: Aloe Vera, Carailli, Mauby Bark, Seed under

leaf

3. **Blood builder:** Black Sage, Log wood, Crattah root, Coconut root

4. **Asthma:**   Wild Calabash (fiddle wood)

5. **Cold remedy:** Snake weed, Dog bush, Christmas bush, Seed under leaf, and Mini Root (Mini Root induces sweating.)

6. **Cools the system:** Water grass, Vervane, love vine (Purr mattress), Cactus (Ratchet)

7. **Biliousness:** Seed-Under-Leaf (Very bitter herb) and Aloe Vera

8. **Sleep inducer:**   Sour-sop bush, Vervane

9. **Expulsion of worms:** Paw-Paw seeds, Vervane, wormgrass, Seed-under-leaf, Aloe Vera

10. **Belly Aches and menstrual pains:** Mayan Roots (very bitter herb), Seed under leaf, Aloe Vera

11. **Cleanser (female reproductive organ):** Caster oil, Crattah root, Seed-under-leaf, and Cassava Grass (The boiled root of Cassava Grass is an excellent remedy for childbearing women.)

12. **Tea bush:**   Santa Maria, Vervane, Lemon grass, Baby bush, Sugar apple bush, Jumbee basil (bush), Christmas bush, Black Sage, Sweet Broom.

13. **Aphrodisiac:**   Branner, Seed under leaf (Also on the reefs lives the Long back—a sea crustacean creature that attaches itself to the rocks. The natives normally ate this delicacy raw. And of course the people's choice Sea Moss)

14. **Carminative:** Senna Pods, aloes, Seed-under-leaf, castor oil

15. **Abortion:** Jumbee basil (bush), Black Sage, and Seed-under-leaf mixed together.

Honorable mention must be given to another local herb that is prevalent in our backyards. Hailed as a food seasoning (condiment), Big leaf thyme, is a herb with antibiotic properties that fights bacteria. It is helpful where cough, bronchitis, asthma, and other respiratory problems exist. It is also a digestive stimulant and is helpful in promoting blood circulation.

The reader will observe from the above list of herbs that Seed-under-leaf and Aloe Vera are the two most commonly mentioned. Although they are far from being called panaceas, they were widely used in every household in Union. It is reputed that Seed-under-leaf is also used for jaundice because it detoxifies the liver; it is also used for hypertension.

The **Trumpet Grass** is another herb that was used regularly during the earlier years when the island did not have a mortuary to preserve a dead body. This herb was not used as an oral medicine but instead was placed on the belly of a dead person to prevent the stomach from rising.

Although the above herbs can be found in every nook and cranny of the island, they have not been used by the most recent generations. Well...they have been used sparingly, at most.

Dry Juice

Unlike the aforementioned medicinal herbs that have their salutary impacts on the population of Union Island, Dry Juice is a relatively common plant that can be seen in any locality on the island. Because it is not known to possess any salutary value, there is no widespread usage of one herb. Jimsonweed, as it is called internationally, can be a source of a powerful hallucinogen, a drug that is capable of producing hallucinations, or changes in the perceptual process.

The Seed under leaf plant

PICKING SALT

Harvesting salt, or salt picking as it is called locally, has been an annual event for the people of Union Island for quite a few centuries. From March to May of every year, the people of Union Island look forward to taking a casual walk on the mud-filled salt pond of Richmond to engage in their rightful obligation of the island's legacy: picking salt.

Because of the semiarid climate of the Grenadines islands, Union Island may experience severe droughts during its annual dry season from December through May. The island has two salt ponds that are situated very close to the shoreline next to mangrove patches. One is located at Ashton Village, south of the island, and hence is called the Ashton salt pond. The other is at Belmont, north and slightly east of the island; it is called the Belmont pond—the only salt producing pond of the island. The Ashton salt pond hasn't produced any significant amount of salt for the past eighty years.

It is during these severe droughts that the sea level descends at alarming rates, which impacts the level of saltwater at these salt ponds, resulting in a wide plane of crystal. Crystal in these ponds at any given point of time is salt that is ready to be harvested. **Picking salt** is the local expression for harvesting this fine product. If the crystal were covered with a thin layer of water, another day or two would be required for that overlying water to evaporate thoroughly. From an aerial prospective, this glittering plane of salt below gives the appearance of a wide football field of diamond; it is a magnificent picture to behold.

The entire country is collectively engaged in this exciting process of reaping this important natural resource. On a good salt-picking day at the Belmond pond, the youngest child to the eldest can be seen physically partaking of this rich legacy. First, there is a twenty- to thirty-foot walk into the muddy pond to reach the line of the salt. You take a container to put the salt into. Always take the size of containers that you can manage when they are filled. Because of the compactness of the mud, the containers remain firmly upright without tilting or overturning even when filled. Most people undertake the task barefoot; others use water boots, in which it is much more difficult to maneuver because of the suction of the mud.

On reaching this wide plane of crystal, the pickers stoop, put both hands together, and open them up, fingers pointing outward and palms facing upward. Then they push gently under the layer of crystal and raise their hands slowly; the salt easily separates from its bond. This process is very easy, requiring little energy. The average size of these layers is 8' x 11' in dimension, and they are composed of numerous fragments that disintegrate like a shattered windshield of a vehicle. These layers of salt are repeatedly placed into the containers or buckets until they are filled. The full containers are then taken back and poured into a large porous bag so that it can be drained of any liquid it may contain. Then off the pickers go again into the pond to collect another container of this valued product. And on it goes.

It is unbelievable how easily these salt crystals can be separated into single blocks of approximately ½-, ¼-, or ¾-inch squares, depending on the thickness of the salt patch. The size of the block of salt increases further into the pond and then decreases again at the end. The color also varies depending on the water content. The whiter the salt is the lower the percentage of water contents.

There was also a small salt pond at Palm Island when the island was uninhabited. Over the years, it has been replaced by commercial infrastructure and businesses.

This salt in these regions is natural sea salt and may be harvested twice per year on a good year. Many years ago, that was the only source of salt the natives had. Today, Unionites can buy packaged, refined salt; it may be much more convenient but can have an adverse effect on their health because of the deficiency of numerous natural elements. It is reputed that eight-two important elements of sea salt have been extracted and sold at exorbitant prices, rendering the salt less effective for good health.

"Natural sea salt, when taken with the consumption of lots of water, will only impact your health positively," says the renowned physician, Dr. Batmanghelidj, internist and cardiologist. It is very important that the natives as well as

90

sufferers of hypertension (high blood pressure) use natural sea salt rather than refined, packaged, iodized salt, which is deficient of its other natural elements. Many hypertension sufferers are inclined to entirely cut off their consumption of salt. However, as Dr. Batmanghelidj also warns, such action is not salutary to the sufferer's health in that it weakens the urinary bladder.

Salt-Picking at Belmont's salt Pond Union Island. (Stanton Gomes)

Chapter Five

EDUCATION AND HOMES

It is safe to say that this island does possess some of the most beautiful homes throughout St. Vincent and the Grenadines. This is not by accident; the people of Union Island love beautiful homes and will go an extra mile to make this possible. If you are on Union Island right now while you are reading this book, chances are, you may have already seen this. Still, take a few minutes to look around you just one more time. The wattle & daub houses of the olden days were also beautiful and well kept.

One of the first board houses built in Union Island was at Ashton; the owner was the late Mrs. Courtney Wilson. This house was located at the corner of the famed Crossroad (Green Corner). Everyone amicably called Mrs. Courtney "Ce Courtney," a form of respect bestowed on folks in their senior years. This structurally intact board house braved numerous hurricanes. Even the noted Hurricane Janet did not do any physical harm to her. She was later razed during the turn of the 21-century. The second board house was also built in Ashton, opposite the first government primary School (Small School). Mr. John Louis Archer, a noted schoolteacher of the Anglican Church School was the owner of this fine structure. Every senior above the age of eighty speaks well of Mr. Archer's teaching capabilities back then.

The government's wall house of Clifton was the first concrete house built on Union Island. Immediately following that was the first concrete house of Ashton, built in 1922. It was built by the late Mr. Allan and Ce Alice Scrubb of Cross-Road. Ba Allan, as he was called, was a much-respected man in the community and had a shop located in the same vicinity. He was the grandfather of Mr. Cecil Scrubb, who resides in America, and Mrs. Icena Wilson, who is currently living at that residence.

It is intriguing to take a few steps back to glimpse what is now referred to as history. The shortage of many facilities on Union Island during her earlier years did not appear to be a significant impediment to the ancestors who had not known any better. Airports, electricity, telephones, and a host of other integral necessities were nonexistent, as were proper health-care centers, pipe-borne water, and adequate roads. One can only imagine what those ancestors may have undergone in severe instances, particularly health-wise. But by and large, they survived with what they had during that time.

The first real institution of transformation was an Anglican Church School that was built around 1875 or a few years earlier. It was situated where the Rectory is now located. The Anglican Church, which was erected in 1875, stands approximately one hundred yards opposite this site.

At the Anglican Church School, the first teacher was Mr. James Donowa, the father of Ada (Hugh's mother). Many years later, Mr. John Louis Archer of Barbados became a teacher of the same institution. Under Mr. Archer's stewardship, the task of teaching several classes were challenging, but he was bent on making his job manageable. He groomed five of his best students to take care of each class while he was teaching one himself. These students became an integral part of the school and were able to conduct classes under his watchful eye. But among his helpers was an exceptional student who had a natural love for mathematics and a desire to lead. Little did he know that this student-helper would later become the most astute entrepreneur the island had ever known? That student was none other than Mr. Augustus "King" Mitchell. Amazingly, he engaged in entrepreneurial service of the people in Union Island—a responsibility that he has held for well over seventy years without reaching the acme of his significantly illustrious career.

During those early years, though the slate was initially used for writing, students were also taught penmanship, and with penmanship, they developed the proper methods of writing. It is of no surprise, then, that older folks, even with their limitations, had excellent handwriting. Take a minute and observe an older folk forming an "S." It is intriguing to observe the pen in motion.

Mr. Archer, who was also in charge of the church, later attained the professional help of two males teachers, namely Mr.

Williams and Mr. Glasgow. After years of service as a pedagogue to the youngsters of Union Island, Mr. Archers lost his wife. It is reputed that she suffered from tuberculosis. Her sister, who was part of the same household, also died as a result of the same ailment. Mr. Archer later married a young Christian girl of the same denomination by the name of Helena. Decades later, in 1931, a decent school was built to replace the deteriorating Anglican Church School. It was erected opposite Mr. Archer's residence at Ashton and was the first government primary school on the land. It was nicknamed "Small School" then, a name that continues even to this day.

This noteworthy Small School has left an indelible mark on the hearts and minds of every Unionite who has sat on those long wooden benches that were once a part of its furniture. Older folks can still remember some of their teachers, who were the first to serve the school. Mr. Williams, Mr. Barlor, Mr. Keen, and Mr. Charles are among the teachers who molded and fashioned many callow minds.

Meanwhile, at Clifton, students attended school at the famed cotton house at Clifton Harbor. The upper floor of this building housed multiple classrooms. This landmark building was later used as the sole revenue office, courtroom, and post office on the island. Then later, the first Clifton Primary School was built; this became a boon to many students of Clifton and nearby areas who had been traveling by foot to the much more adequate school at Ashton. In December 1995, the old cotton house was destroyed by fire; this rendered the island devoid of its already sparse database and a vital historical landmark.

The Ashton Primary School at Clifton Road was built in 1957 and served both communities for numerous years. Then in early 1971, the construction of Union Island Junior Secondary School was completed; it was made available to the first batch of students in September of that year. One year later (i.e., September 1972), another two classes entered; they were Form 1A & B. A month later, on October 24, the ribbon was cut by the late Princess Margaret to officially open the secondary school. She was the younger sister of Queen Elizabeth II of England. Like Tommy Hilfiger and Mick Jagger, she owned property on the neighboring cay of Mustique Island. Princess Margaret, a mother of two, later died on February 9, 2002, six months short of her seventy-second birthday.

The education system that is adopted from England had a stranglehold on all of the British Caribbean islands. In the early twentieth century, the school structure of Union Island was just about taking shape, and that led to an education evolution. Later, with the accessibility of secondary education in Union Island, students no longer had to attend schools at St. Vincent to better their education. But amid all the refinements that now contribute to the educational transformation in Union Island, the schools of long ago had their flaws. Today, a young female student can be an expectant mother and still remain comfortable in the classroom with her classmates. In the past, that would have been considered an egregious crime. If a teenage woman were to be found in such situation, she will have to kiss her school days good-bye; even if she exhibited the wherewithal necessary for a productive academic future, she would have still been expelled nonetheless. This action had put an end to many young careers in a system void of alternatives. Because of the indignity that was attached to this seemingly indecent act, young women who realized they were pregnant wittingly abandoned the classrooms rather than to face the embarrassment of expulsion.

During the older days, no one wanted a student to take the wrong path in life, so they did not spare the rod (applicable corporal punishment). Not only the parents of that child but also by any parent in that community practiced this method of discipline. This form of discipline was further extended to every teacher of that day, and the leather belt was often the authority of choice. The male student was much more likely to feel the belt on his behind or on the palm of his hand than females, who were viewed as delicate and undeserving of this kind of chastisement. However, a few could not escape, especially if they exhibited any masculine characteristics. A student's shirt out of his pants, tardiness, cutting school (playing hooky), and insubordination were issues that warranted the use of the strap. Again, those were the days of yesterday; today, the customs are quite different, fortunately...I meant unfortunately.

Union Island Junior Secondary School came into being in 1972 and was a timely venture that has since given rise to a much higher level of learning. It also provided employment for the yearly graduating students who were fresh out of the schools from St. Vincent and needed some form of employment. It also provided employment for the yearly graduating students who were fresh out of the schools from St. Vincent and needed some form of employment. Returning students from St. Vincent, such as Audlyn, Christine, Dillon, Umlyn, Renrick, Edison, Nadine, and the late Denzil Stewart were able to attain employment as first-time teachers. Mickey Hutchinson, who completed his studies Trinidad & Tobago, was another young vibrant teacher. They all did an exemplary job in rendering their services to the little island. But then came the inevitable, like a pull of gravity. Unfortunately, they, like many others, have succumbed to the forceful enticement of The Exodus Factor, making the United States, Canada, and elsewhere their homes.

A WOMAN'S ROLE YESTERDAY

The women in early communities had diverse responsibilities. In Union Island, the average size of a family was eight members. The wives were solely responsible for the upbringing of their offspring. They had to wash, starch, and iron the clothes as well as cook, clean, garden, do the dishes, and shop. And all of the above were done on time to keep a functional home. Not to mention that these wives' circumstances were filled with the usual, sometimes overwhelming stresses associated with being a mother, doctor, nurse, teacher, arbitrator in sibling rivalries, wife, and lover—and the responsibility of satisfying their husbands at all costs.

These young women of grace and beauty were vibrant and strong both physically and emotionally.

Unfortunately, any desire to excel academically was fervently met with disapproval from their husbands, and if, before marriage, a woman held a job as a teacher or public servant, they were discouraged from doing so upon entering the marriage. So it is safe to say that the woman's role as a wife concluded her educational advancement, but brought on enormous responsibilities with great self-denial. Her principal role was childbearing, parenting, and all of the attributes of a housewife.

Those responsibilities of our grandmothers, mothers, aunts, and sisters were tedious compared to those of the marriages of today. Our patriarchs were to bring home the bacon, which they did dutifully on most occasions. However, the husband provided little to no help to his mate with the endless household burden that was bestowed on her by tradition. Nevertheless, an amicable marriage relationship remained intact for an average of more than six decades, indicating that the woman honored the phrase "till death do us part." The question must now be posed: Is the women of today willing to emulate the women of yesterday in regards to the enormous responsibilities placed on their shoulders? Many will respectfully Think otherwise.

Having said all of the above, I feel obligated to mention the matriarch I have known throughout my entire existence on this planet. I use the word matriarch because she exemplifies the true meaning of motherhood. She is the stem wall, the pillar of the home, my strength yesterday and even more so today because of what she permanently ingrained in me.

I can say emphatically that she is largely responsible for whom I am and what I am becoming. I honestly do not think there is another person who truly knows the might of this soft-spoken woman as much as I do. To me, my mother, Sheila Roache-Stewart, epitomizes the rock of Gibraltar. She has been such a great inspiration to us. She raised us with sheer determination and hard work, and she believed strongly in herself and in the methods she implemented while raising us. As a youngster growing up, I always looked up to her, not only because she fed, clothed, and kept us soundly within the guidelines of ethics and morality, but also because her presence meant the world to us. And let's face it-does anyone really loves you the way your mother does? The answer here may be relative, but I can say categorically that she was my first love because of the love that I received from her in abundance. She also has been the first hero and role model in my life. And for this I can state emphatically that the best in me I owe to her.

In looking back at her total contribution to my life, I inadvertently aspired to seeing those kinds of qualities in my relationships with females with whom I shared my affections, but to no avail. That is how much she affected my life; she left a greater indelible mark on me than on any of my siblings. Today I am experiencing a void in my life here in Brooklyn, New York, because I am unable to implement some of the customs and traditions that had richly made my life worthy in the Caribbean. Sheila, to this day, is very passionate with her agriculture and animal husbandry, which she does dutifully every day. She rears her sheep, goats, and fowl right in her backyard with fervent passion and exhibits the same desire that she has always had since I have known her.

I mentioned earlier that we had a large herd of goats stationed at the pastures of Ms. Irene —by far the largest herd on the island. Sheila was responsible for this creation and was one of the most noteworthy agricultural farmers of her time in Campbell.

Thank you, Sheila; I love you dearly!

YESTERDAY'S MARRIAGE

Now let us carefully follow the steps of a typical marriage of good old yesterday.

A young man sees the woman of his liking or dreams and desires to make her his wife. To make this a reality, he must immerse himself in marital traditions. Dating is short-lived at all costs, for all roads hastily lead to the altar, the tying of the knot, the marriage.

The first step is to inform the parents of the prospective bride that he has an interest in their daughter. This is done by visiting the home of the parents on a late evening to disclose his affection for the young lady and his intent to take her hand in marriage. Writing a letter that asks their approval of his marriage to their daughter also does it. Now some parents will go so far as to select mates for their children without first consulting the children. In this particular situation, the parents of the prospective bride and groom subsequently develop a closer rapport among themselves. In many cases, the parents of sons may go as far as to become a watchdog over the prospective young lady to protect their son's interest.

Now in some cases a young man and woman may meet and express affinity toward each other. But when this does not meet the approval of some parents (mostly the son's), who may be prejudiced against the girl and her family, the parents may express disapproval of his intent. They might fear that he will disparage himself by marrying into a lesser family. This may take place in the girl's family as well, especially if the young man doesn't seem to have much financial security. The parents of yesterday had a lot of clout regarding the choices that their children made; that's the way it was then. And even today, if we look carefully, we may spot some residual impact. Because of this parental issue, many young couples were dissuaded from relationships during their early years but later reunited after they had experienced the turmoil of unsuccessful marriages. Many many older men in particular can attest to that.

The process of visiting the home of the young lady or writing a letter to ask her parents' permission to take their daughter's hand in marriage is locally called "going home" for that particular person.

Some young men were confident enough to go to her parents and request her hand in marriage without the young woman being aware of their intentions. Others who were a bit squeamish or did not have the self-confidence would seek the assistance of a noteworthy person in the community to accompany them to the parents' home.

In rare cases, if a young man who sailed on national bulk liners was called out to sea before he could approach the parents, he might write a letter to communicate his intentions. The approval of the parents (liner employees were hardly ever denied) brought closure to one chapter. He was now privileged to call on the young woman at home and to occasionally take her out on a walk to the beach.

The logical step that follows is the official engagement as the courtship picks up momentum. Next, an engagement ring is placed on the finger of the bride-to-be. This is done in the presence of family members and a few close friends. During such time, the parents of the prospective bride amicably inform the suitor in no uncertain term that the engagement term will be brief. Consequently, all plans and arrangements for the wedding intensify, and the momentum again shifts into higher gear. With little time to waste, a date is set for that big day. The onus of responsibility now rests on the shoulders of the prospective bride and groom's parents. The choice of wedding gown and outfits for the groom, bridesmaid, chief bridesmaid, flower girl, honor attendant, bride's escort, best man, and officiant (minister or priest) must be put into place. So must also be the flowers and seating arrangements, cake, and the big cookouts to feed the community. Welcome to the institution of marriage.

The groom-to-be honors tradition by voluntarily refraining from seeing his prospective bride for the seven days leading up to the wedding. The day that precedes the wedding marks the first of a pair of cookouts for such a momentous undertaking. "The Parents Plate" is done at the home of the groom where the parents express generosity of the highest order. A cow, goats, sheep, pigs, and fowls may be slaughtered to provide enough food to feed the community for the entire day. Cooking is done in huge copper pots placed on three stones while firewood is used as energy to fuel the fires. Elaborate cooking and dancing fills the atmosphere with glee as residents descend on the home to celebrate this forthcoming event. Singing erupts in anticipation of a long, happy marriage for the bride and groom. This local song sung in the African dialect is surely a favorite for the occasion. A faction of the huge gathering sings a question while another faction responds, also in singing. It is sung and danced with the beat of the African drum.

Ah we want peace and unity
All ah we ah wan
Ah we want peace and unity
All ah we ah wan
Ah we want peace and unity

All way mama want?
Mama want peace and unity
All way Mama want?
Mama want peace and unity

All way ah we want?
Ah we want peace and unity
All way ah we want?
Ah we want peace and unity
All way ah we want?

Ah we, which means "all we" in the old dialect of Union Island, is interpreted in clear English as "all of us."

The African drum again rolls as the West African customs resurface and is expressed once again through dancing and singing.

Open the door leh me man come in
All ah we ah one famileee............
Open the door leh me man come in
All ah wee ah one family.

This gala, which offers much to eat and drink as well as lots of laughter, extends far into the night. While the kerosene lamps are lit inside of the house, the flambeau or massantow are ablaze outside, providing light for the event through the dark of

Night, until sunset.

The day of the wedding is the birth of a new celebration. The location will now be at the bride's home, where cooking commences just after sunrise and is accompanied by other activities. The points of interest that precede the actual tying of the knot are the "Meeting Up" or the "Dancing of the Cake."

On the day of the wedding, very early in the morning, the families of both the bride and the groom convene at a central location with a large following of spectators on site to witness this grand event. Cultural music begins with the beat of the African drum while designated dancers take center stage to exhibit their prowess. These dancers are elegantly adorned, with long, wide, frilly floral skirts that lend mobility and grace to their dexterity. The large gathering of spectators surrounds the continuous dancing and singing but gives ample room to the dancers. The crowd is almost wild now as the decorated mothers of both bride and groom assert themselves at center stage; this is a true expression of the island's culture. With the mothers becoming the center of focus, all eyes are glued on them.

A competition ensues as fierce dancing among the two begins. This is rightfully referred as the Meeting Up. The mothers of the bride and groom firmly grab the right and left sides of their skirts and motioned them in and out, up and down with reckless abandon. This is followed by sensual whining by both females, bringing the activity to a point of culmination. The spectators themselves are unstoppable as they repetitively sing the favorite two-lined song. The first line, sung as the question, is posed, "All way ah we want?" Then the second part is an ecstatic response: "Ah we want peace and unity." The heat is so intense that some excited onlookers are provoked to join the dancers at center stage, but are restrained. This is the heart of this gathering and sets the tone for the eventual wedding ceremony later during the day.

Almost as soon as the whining simmers to a snail's pace, two dancers emerge with wooden trays on their heads. These wooden trays are placed on a firmly wrapped or folded cloth positioned under the trays on the heads of these female dancers. They dance elegantly with these trays balanced on their heads; hands almost glued to their waists and never seeming to be uncomfortable though their prized possessions are unattended.

This artistic skill that is bequeathed from West Africa is a practice that is common in Union Island. Heavy loads are carried in baskets, trays, buckets, and so on by balancing them on their heads—which African women attest is by far the best way to carry their heaps. The locals call the cloth that cushions the weight of the object on the head an "Akartne," though it is called Karta in Union. The contents of these embellished trays on their heads are the wedding cakes and their fine adornments of flowers. These cakes were baked and decorated ahead of time for this significant event. While the cake of the bride is highly decorated with multiple layers, that of the groom remains a single layer, according to the dictates of tradition.

The dancers of the cake must now make way for the final episode of the morning, the dancing of the flag. The fingers of the drummers are never too tired to evoke the sound of the African drum, whose beat reflects the regularity of a metronome. The presence of these final two dancers of the flags epitomizes the authenticity of the culture from the motherland. Two flags are held aloft on entrance and waved rhythmically to the beat of the drums. It is done with such dexterity that one might assume that a sword fight was about to develop. This dancing continues at center stage as the flag bearers circle the ring several times and then stop abruptly. The poles of the flags are then carefully placed across each other, forming an X while the flags themselves are turned toward each other. The male flag lies on top of the female's flag; this exemplifies dominance of the man or submissiveness of his mate. This of course is ritualistic in scope and has its salutary significance. Such vibrant activity marks the end of the morning session, which lasts approximately one hour.

The crowds disperse at the end of the dance while some members descend at the home of the bride's family. It is another big day of cooking, and everyone is eager to do his or her part to make this event a success. Everything that has been planned from the initial evening visit by the prospective son-in-law to the marital ceremony must now come to fruition. Every effort is geared toward this event being impeccable. From here on, everything that transpires into the actual marriage resembles that of a typical Christian marriage. Therefore, we will stop here, for nothing beyond this point is unusual. Till death do us part? **I do!**

With the completion of the marital bond, the niceties, and the novel experiences, it is safe to surmise that, in a few months, the young bride will be in the family way. The parents of the married couple again take on the responsibility of guardianship; the dos and don'ts are handed down in such a way as to leave no alternative. The young couple, having no experience, does nothing but accede to every word of command. The months are swiftly flying by. It is now seven, eight months and the pregnancy is quite visible. As with the wedding, elaborate preparation is made for the unborn. Someone unfamiliar with the culture might be baffled as to which or how many of the females are pregnant. These precautionary measures are the action of overly concerned mothers and in-law; nevertheless, everyone means well.

Thus, a youngster becomes part of a new generation in a population that must succumb to the metamorphosis that has become a culture in Union Island.

THE STEWART'S FAMILY

Numerous natives have been mentioned who bear the ever-present family name STEWART. It is common knowledge that the Stewart family is the largest in Union Island—much larger than any other family. But how did that happen when the Spann family was widely established and recognized from its inception? The Mulzac family, who for most part supplanted the Spann, was at one time the chief architects on the island as well as the principal entrepreneurs, shipwrights, boat owners, and landowners. They, too, are meager in numbers today compared to yesterday when the onus of government in Union Island was squarely on their shoulders.

The Stewart family name is by no means an African name; it is of English origin, as are the many family names that Unionites have been carrying for centuries. Studies have shown that Stewart is an occupational name for a steward or manager of a household or estate, or one who had charge of a king's or important noble's household. These names were given to us during slavery. Though not by our own choice, we bear the names of our slave masters with pride. It is important that we now study the roots or origins of the numerous names that we are identified by. We should also have a thorough understanding of their meanings. It is equally important that we recognize that our ancestors were stolen from Africa, so we have basically lost our way. In jeopardy since our exodus from the motherland, we have lost our names, languages, religion, culture, folkways, mores, and norms. Nevertheless, we have earned the right of ownership after 250 years of existence on Union Island.

The patriarch of the Stewart family was Mr. McDowell Stewart, a sharecropper who had firsthand experience as a slave and quite a number of children to begin with. As with numerous ancestors of his time, there is no documentation available to indicate the date of his birth. Mr. McDowell and his wife, Louisiana Wilson begat quite a number of children back then. Some of their names were Robert, Peter, John, Aaron, Emanuel, Hughwith, Violet, Artine, and Vashtie. They were the generation of first landowners; it was during that time that the British Crown subdivided the island, giving the residents the pride of ownership. During this time, the cotton crop, still the main source of income was grown throughout the island. But corn and pigeon peas had already made a mark, and later supplanted it to become the chief crops on the island, and it has remained so even until today. Corn and peas are further discussed in another part of the book.

The proliferous nature of these descendants of Africa was evident throughout Union Island, especially in the Stewart families. The children of Mc. Dowell Stewart had an average of nine children apiece—except Emanuel, whose count was in the vicinity of twenty-plus. So like Jacob of the Bible, they fathered lots of children who were undoubtedly their pride and joy. The Stewart families were very close-knitted and valued bloodline as sacred. Committed to making life better, young men took to both the land and sea to take care of their families. The women, being housewives and mothers, remained true to the use of the land. They were very supportive of their husbands in making life possible and honored the phrase "Till death do us part."

Although the mass exodus of young men from Union Island during the turn of the twentieth century and onward affected the population tremendously, the Stewart influence was still significant. There were three major concentrations of Stewart families on the island. The central village of Ashton all the way to Bordeaux was where one concentration was found; second was the land at Campbell Village, occupied by the descendants of Charles "Mindo" Stewart. Then finally there was Richmond, with some descendants of John Henry Stewart.

As mentioned before, the high level of fertility was not exclusive to the Stewart families; many other families were there too. Other families who made up Union Island's population were named Wilson, Scrubb, Douglas, John, Hutchinson, Roache, Ambrose, Jones, Simmons, Alexander, James, Paul, Regis, Harvey, and Daniel. The whole of Union Island is intertwined enough that it is said locally, "All ah we ah one family" (We are all one family).

As with the Spann and Mulzac families, these huge concentrations of Stewarts have diminished considerably, especially in recent years. This, of course, is a result of The Exodus Factor. With that being said, it is safe to surmise that the dilution of the Stewart's bloodline will give rise to another family name—maybe before this book is published. Only time will tell.

♦♦♦□*Chapter six*

FRED HEMCEED

In the village of Campbell lived a middle-aged man named Frederick Hempseed. His neighbors called him Fred. Fred lived alone in a white stone house with a dog he called Ned. Stones are bountiful on Union Island, especially in the district of Campbell. Fred's house was built during the 1960s, when concrete houses supplanted the previously wattle and daub and board houses that had been pervasive throughout the Grenadines. The natives sometimes referred to them as thatch houses.

Wattle and daub houses on Union Island were built of a mesh of woven sticks and vines chiefly acquired from the rich mangrove vegetation that lies endlessly along the coastline. These meticulously woven sticks and vines are skillfully smeared with mud—a combination of cattle dung and a special type of dirt that is proportionately mixed into a dough-like paste that possesses great bonding capability. One location of Union Island where the most suitable soil was found for building these houses was in the vicinity of the late Mrs. Mo and Kent Hutchinson at Clifton Road. In essence, the wattle supplies the mesh, and of course the daub is the mud. The roofs of these villas were made primarily of grass, making these small shelters amazingly attractive. Again, these were the first dwellings on Union Island, and of course they speak well of the ancestors' skills in creating stuff of astonishing complexity.

Now, Mr. Fred was a loner who was not hesitant to have a drink or two, but he liked the company of young boys. He was one of those cunning, deceptive recluses who really enjoyed and took advantage of the liberty that existed on this pristine and unspoiled cay. He never wore a hat; he thought it was too hot to cover his head in a hot, tropical island such as Union. He walked along the beach early each morning and looked up at the clouds. Once I heard him say, "Rainbow in the morning is fishermen's warning, but rainbow in the night is shepherd's delight." He was staring at a rainbow that morning.

Many times he mentioned that his homeland was Ireland, but he said nothing in detail. He did not speak with an Irish accent, which makes me now wonder where this short white man was really from. *"Row, row, row your boat gently down the street, merely, merely, merely, merely life is but a dream,"* he would sing under his breath. He never talked about his friends and family back in Ireland, but he mentioned he had a daughter or a niece; I cannot quite remember exactly which it was. I can remember clearly these two words that he uttered repeatedly: Sapoo Fay and Gadiloo. That's exactly how they were pronounced, but they were foreign words. I did not know what language it was. Sapoo Fay, he said, meant "What to do?" I would sometimes listen to what he had to say while my father would so often engage him in conversation while we were on our journey to take care of our animals. We reared a lot of animals deep in the bushes of Ms. Irene's, and we had more than one hundred. We were proud farmers, and although I was relatively small then, being the second son of my family, I was deemed the principal caretaker of our large herd.

I was a part of almost all the activities and decision making at home. I had multiple responsibilities. They trusted me so much that I felt I was obligated to perform way above the abilities of my siblings, and I was expected to not make the mistakes that my siblings made. This perception was a disadvantage, as I began to look at my life very seriously, and would later rebel in my early twenties. I would exhibit high levels of defiance when I thought that my rights were challenged.

The onus of responsibility was squarely on my shoulders, and the weight of accountability affected me both positively and negatively; I am now a perfectionist and can spend painstaking amounts of time to get a job done, even if it may be daunting and extremely challenging. The negative is that I may expect total commitment from others who, by today's standards, may not possess that level of tenacity. I later learned from the renowned English author Dr. Samuel Johnson, who wrote, "As I know more of mankind I expect less of them. I am ready now to call a man a good man upon easier terms than I was formerly."

That surely mitigates the stress of expecting too much from others; it renders a bit of solace.

But who was this man called Mr. Fred Hempseed? Was that really his name? What would cause someone—a foreigner, for that matter, to leave the comfort of his country of origin to make the most southerly island of St. Vincent and the Grenadines his home? A third-world country at that. An island that was deficient of nightlife, void of electricity, telephones, and even the hope of having a television to connect with the outside world. Transistor radios at that time were our only means of communication with the outside world, and amazingly, this man never looked back at his country, not even for a vacation.

There were neither proper medical facilities nor hospitals to handle the sick; anyone who succumbed to a serious illness was transported by boat to the mainland for medical services. Fred did not have a wife or children, and he surely did not have a woman or a girlfriend. He did not come to Union Island as an entrepreneur, nor was he a part of any philanthropic or altruistic organizations. He did not possess any of the qualities that would have rendered him productive at his new abode.

Because he was not personable, no one expected him to be community oriented, for he was never a part of any social gathering and was seldom seen as a spectator of any of our local sports on the island. He really kept a low profile. He was abnormally reticent, and that may have been the best thing for him to be. He was totally out of sight, for lack of a better word. Being a recluse kept him from being under any possible surveillance.

No one knew enough about him to speak of Mr. Fred Hempseed at length, so they did not. So this question must be asked again and again. Who was this man? A stranger he was in the legal sense, yet the government of that day did not question his presence and could not care less, for that matter. It is believed that he was not a resident of St. Vincent and the Grenadines, but was amicably accepted by the people of Union Island, who were overly humanistic by nature. To the older folks, he was their neighbor. They treated him as their own, and he exhibited neighborly responsibilities as well. He had huge water tank, a cistern, and he was never hesitant to give a couple buckets of water to his immediate neighbors during the almost ubiquitous dry season that has plagued Union Island from the time of the ancestors even until now.

Mr. Fred has been deceased some thirty years, buried at Ashton Cemetery on May December 7, 1981. He occupies a space among the graves of the ancestors. His tombstone states that he was born May 2, 1902. Unfortunately, we may never know who Mr. Fred Hempseed really was, whether he was a fugitive—as was said of John Donaldson by two white couples, a mercenary, or just another peaceful and humble resident. Many are a bit dubious about the latter; his scars and sealed left ear spoke voluminously of his former life outside of Union Island somewhere on another frontier. Only heaven knows.

WAS HIS NAME JOHN DONALDSON?

It was on a quiet Sunday afternoon at Basin Beach. Usually on a day like that, one would expect the Baptist church to be loudly singing "Tell me, how you did feel when your sins were washed away," as they prepare to baptize another convert. That afternoon I was walking the beach alone when two white couples, gracious in their approach, asked me my name, age, where I lived, the whole nine yards. I eagerly acceded to their request and even divulged more information than they requested. Immediately, they became fond of me, and I was comfortable, too, so I asked them if they had sailed all the way from America to Union with a yacht. They did not tell me that they were from America; I just surmised that most white folks were from America.

At the secondary school that I was attending, we had an American teacher by the name of Ms. Helen E. Hunt, so I went on to talk about her because she, too, was from America. Now I should have been at Sunday school by then, but much time had already passed, and if I'd had any intention of going to Sunday school, I should have been home at least two hours earlier. But I had already planned out my afternoon, and Sunday school at Gospel Hall Church was surely out of my roster. To make matters worse, I was enjoying the company of those white folks. It was much better than listening to Brother Lenox (Sunday-school teacher) for two Sundays in a row.

But as the hours passed, I began to feel on edge. I felt it was time to go home, but at least I had a worthwhile excuse to give my parents as to why I was not at home in time for Sunday school. Just before I left their company, one female asked me, "Do you know John Donaldson? "Yes," I replied, once again engaged and ready to spew the contents of my guts. "He has a goat that eats money—a big goat," I continued in elation.

"His name is not John Donaldson," she replied as she fixed her stare on me. "He is a fugitive." She was rather contemplative.

"What is his name?" I asked. They all smiled but never responded to my question. "What is his name?" I bellowed in excitement again and again but to no avail. At this time, I guessed that I had outstayed my welcome—but in fact; they were enjoying every moment of my presence and my dialect as much as I enjoyed their company. "He is a fugitive," the other female replied again as I prepared to leave. I bid farewell and left immediately as the sun crept its way toward the horizon.

It was not a bad day at all I thought, as I got closer to home. "His name is not John Donaldson, and he is a fugitive?" I continued asking myself repeatedly.

These two statements aroused curiosity in my mind, but I did not know what to make of them. I did not know what the word fugitive meant, either, but the little old Oxford Concise Dictionary, being the only dictionary at home, became the final authority. I was not in the mood to discuss with my parents what those white folks had told me, nor was I in any hurry to relate to my friends or siblings what I had heard. I thought that Mr. John Donaldson was still living in Union Island at that time and did not know what all of this meant. Little did I know that those two statements I'd heard would give rise to unanswered questions that would puzzle me for many years. Still today, after almost forty years, the best I can do is to make conjectures.

Helen Hunt, as I mentioned earlier, was one of two teachers sent to us from Canada as a humanitarian gesture; this information came through the grapevine of informal communication. Later, we were told that these two teachers were from the United States of America.

Ms. Helen Hunt and Mr. Mike G. Carville were excellent teachers. They started as teachers at the Union Island Junior Secondary School on June 5, 1973. My classmates and I later learned that they were Peace Corps volunteers. Whatever that was, it surely did not mean too much to us then, for we were wrapped up in the art of learning. Ms. Hunt taught language arts while Mr. Carville was responsible for mathematics. The discipline that Ms. Hunt taught us in class has influenced me so profoundly that it has stayed with me even until today. Mr. Carville was subtle and less imposing.

Mr. Mike G. Carville was well versed in teaching

mathematics, and the method that he employed was well received. The name of our class was Form 2A, and by now and we were doing extremely well, but as the saying goes, "All good things must come to an end." Indeed the end was closer than any of us had anticipated. Ms. Hunt married the aforementioned John Donaldson after a short time—maybe less than one year. Mr. Donaldson established a construction company, bought land, and built houses that provided off-and-on employment for some of our local contractors. I had seen Mr. Donaldson but once, and that afternoon he appeared drunk. That afternoon he came to Crossroad with a big ram goat. Some of the kids at the time were saying that the goat ate money, and that was appealing to me as a youngster.

He had two daughters, Kate and Kathryn. Kate was the younger sister. We attended the same school during her stay on Union Island; she was my classmate.

Shortly after Ms. Hunt became Mrs. Donaldson, Mr. Carville left his teaching job at the school to work at the Ministry of Finance in St. Vincent, or, so they say. He never returned to Union Island after that and was never seen by his students again.

Although there are many charitable organizations that welcome people who truly desire to reach out to the less fortunate, and many good people do volunteer to devote a year, several years, or even their entire life to work overseas among the needy; it must be questioned whether it was the true intension of these two people to volunteer their services in a third-world country? Again, some of the same questions raised about Mr. Fred Hempseed in another chapter might be asked about these two people. Why would they confine themselves to a lesser standard of living than what they could attain in the great US of A? During such time, they were not offered housing and living conditions commensurate with the life that they were accustomed to in their homeland. This is not to speak disparagingly about Union Island in any way, fashion, or form. This is just the unadulterated truth. Being candid and ingenuous is just in good keeping with integrity.

Ms. Hunt's stay in Union Island from that point on was short-lived; she, too, left quietly. Her husband also disappeared.

It was reputed that a yacht came near where he had built

his house and abducted him. This is an area where he was said to be living quietly, if not peacefully. If Mr. Donaldson was indeed abducted or forcefully removed from his residence, then we must question by whom? Was the government of St. Vincent and the Grenadines aware of what was taking place in Little Tahiti at that time? Unfortunately, Mr. Donaldson was never heard of or seen again. The vast acreage of land where Mr. Donaldson once lived in the vicinity of the Richmond, Union Island, now bears his name, with no negative connotations attached to it.

Some folks said that after spending many years in her homeland, Mrs. Helen E. Hunt / Donaldson finally returned to visit Union Island one last time.

UNEXPLAINED

Since my family and I have been living at Campbell, (1968) it was common knowledge that one day there would be a paved road leading from Campbell to the pastures of Ms. Irene. We were also told that this road would eventually extend all the way around Union Island. We were accustomed to the use of numerous tracks to take us almost everywhere we wanted to go, and our legs were our principal and only means of transportation. These tracks were rocky, thorny, and unfriendly to our bare feet. We had to contend with irritating leaves of the Burn Bush, Stinger Nettle, and the notorious Red Man Blood (Thorny plant) the leaves lay camouflaged amongst the numerous dry leaves during the severe dry season. The thorns of the Burn Bush are clear crystal, so when one is pricked with this notorious plant, there is no need to make an effort to extract those seemingly colorless needles; it is best to leave the needles where they are. The needles of the Burn Bush plant exude not only a burning sensation but also a highly agitating itch that irritates for a long period of time.

So yes, we were excited about hearing our parents and other natives talk about the paved road coming into fruition; we now had something to hope for, a dream. This proposed new road would be a replica of the existing roads, which consisted of two-lane tracks or wheel strips that ran parallel to each other. That was the most economical means for the government to provide viable roads on the island during those early years. These lanes were meant for the tires of motor vehicles, most notably the jeep, which was the first means of vehicular transportation on the island during the early 1960s. So this proposed new road would have been a boon, enabling us to use a vehicle when necessary, but more importantly, to ride our bicycles from our homes all the way to the pastures of Ms. Irene where our goats were tied and kept.

We had quite a few animals to take care of: goats, sheep, cows, pigs, chickens, and ducks were a few of the many animals that were part of our daily responsibilities. The latter three were reared at home. In fact, we were involved in the largest animal husbandry on the island during those earlier years, hence we were never buyers of fresh meat, poultry, or even fish.

Being a kid and expecting a road in rural areas did engender a bit of excitement. I had my plan concocted and in place, for I had been looking at my father's old bicycle for a very long time. I intended to use it as soon as the road was put into place. Unfortunately, this road never materialized as anticipated, but surprisingly, what transpired two years later was so baffling that it left me confounded for many, many years to come. The idea of writing this book had been on my mind for quite a long time—since I was nineteen years old. However, the impetus for getting on my computer to make Union Island Then and Now a reality essentially stemmed from this imprisoned story that I am now about to set free.

It was a beautiful day; the clouds were high in the sky. I guess they were cumulonimbus if my memory serves me correctly. Change was in the air -something seemed to be happening. At 4:30 P.M., my brother Urias and I were on our journey to the bushes of Ms. Irene to take care of the numerous goats and cows. We had just come in sight of Mr. Fred Hempseed's house when we saw two small jeeps parked with their keys still in their ignitions. That drew our attention, but we had to hasten our travel to Ms. Irene's pastures before darkness set in.

On Union Island, and on all the Caribbean islands for that matter, the sun always set early. Six o' clock and it would be pitch-black. Nevertheless, we were on our way when we observed that work was being done on the road. Excavation, tree removal, boulders, and so on were in progress. We were tempted to stop and look, but the sun's haste to get to the horizon was enough to deter our puerile affinity for folly. So we went by hastily, took care of the animals, and returned quickly. It was evident in our minds that we were not going to be thorough in taking care of the animals that afternoon. We glanced at each other, and that tacit message was fully communicated. We returned to the worksite, and there were three white men still working. But they did not stay much longer, for they had done quite a bit earlier that day and were just about ready to retire after a hard day's work.

The following day, two others accompanied the three

white men. They cleared the road rather quickly, almost to the Devi-Devi tree that overlooked Basin's beach. It would take another two days to get to Basket, a local pond that we used to supply drinking water for our animals. Wells were pervasive throughout the island, but none were available at such an altitude.

The clearing of the much-anticipated road continued, but instead of continuing where the old track existed, it made a sudden ninety-degree angle just before it got to the pond. That raised concern to my brother and me, for this road, did not appear to be going where the old road existed, which was where we reared our animals. This road ran another 120 meters through the dense bushes east of Basket Pond and then took a sudden right turn 140 meters up to a small hill. This hill overlooks Basin Beach and the entire coastal area, which encompassed Queensbury Point, Frigate Rock, Carriacou, Petit Martinique, Petit St. Vincent, and Palm Island (Prune), and it offered a clear but partial view of the Clifton Harbor. From there, one can see almost every marine activity without being seen.

Though there was limited manpower and minimal machinery for such a gigantic task, the clearing of the road went quickly. Vehicles were driven all the way to the top of the hill now; the hill is known as Fort Basin. It is situated near a plot of land owned by Ms. Izolyn, Zennie's mother (mentioned earlier). By then, she was an old woman who lived up the Village of Muddy Street, or Pauper-Land as it was called during those early days. Rumor had it that those white folks were going to build a house at the top of the hill. The hill was cut clear of its vegetation, giving more reason to believe that a structure was imminent on that particular site. What was a bit intriguing in retrospect is that I have never observed any person of authority from Union Island or St. Vincent visiting that site or giving it any form of approval.

In my observation, not one adult engaged those folks in any conversation. Every adult I knew who was present during that time acted as though they were consumed with other social issues that did not allow them time to do anything else. Most were rather standoffish, as though it were out of bounds to even venture near those guys. It was a tacit feeling of acquiescence that we, the natives, exhibited toward most foreign folks. It always made me feel out of pace. But this attitude was so pervasive in the community that any action or inaction contrary to the folkways or customs would have stood out negatively like a sore thumb. To look back now at this and other similar experiences, I can genuinely say that the institution of slavery had its profound impact on us then, and even to this day. These folks did not say too much to us despite the fact that we were kids who could not resist the temptation of satisfying our probing eyes.

That new road provided easier access to other grazing pastures. We sometimes rotated from pasture to pasture, giving one exhausted area ample time to replenish itself with fresh grass. On the new concrete road, the logical step to follow would have been placing a layer of well-orchestrated concrete capped with a layer of pitch. After all, it was in the hands of white folks, and in our minds much was expected of them. If anyone could have done the best job, it would have been white folks. Or so we thought.

In the late afternoon and into the night, these white men remained in the bushes with backpacks but never gave the impression that they were strangers. They knew exactly what they were doing. They were on a mission and were accomplishing their mission quickly. Then suddenly, two local masons built a small concrete shed with a galvanized roof. It was located close to the coastline of Basin Beach but in an inconspicuous area. The sand for building the structure was collected at the nearby beach. Those were the years when residents had the privilege of using bayside sand for all their construction. That privilege has since been taken away because it only does harm to the land that is already susceptible to sea erosion.

Basin Beach is an almost isolated, beautiful beach of Campbell where lots of boats and small vessels came in unnoticed from other islands with foodstuffs, liquor, and other valuable commodities without having to pay tariffs or excise duties. These boats would come in late in the evening laden with products, spend approximately two hours there, and then disappear to another location. This was a long-time custom that helped many shop owners to escape the enormous taxes that the government charges.

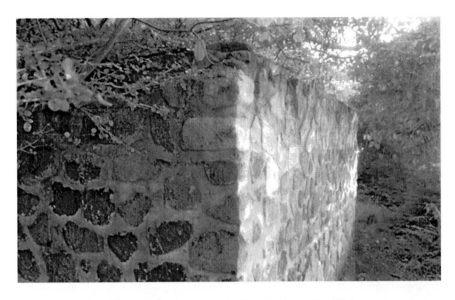

The remains of a safe haven at Basin beach. This was once a valuable repository. As seen here, it was well built then and is still structurally intact now, after forty years.

This form of illegal trade was not exclusive to Union Island. Nevertheless, it is believed that this method of evading customs with contraband escalated into drug trafficking on a large scale.

About a week later (1973), after the construction of the shed, my brother Urias and I left home on a Saturday night at 8 PM. with a flambeau / massantow and caucus bag, to catch crabs in the lower area of Campbell. A massantow is a bottle with a narrow mouth, (a wine bottle) half filled with kerosene, and plugged tightly with a cloth extending approximately four inches into the bottle while another inch and a half protrudes out of the bottle to be lit by fire. While the fire is lighting, the bottle is tilted every ten minutes so that the kerosene can provide fuel to the fire. Though this may be considered primitive by today's standards, it was an effective method of providing a sustainable glow of light during those dark nights when electricity was only a figment of the imagination. It efficiently provided light for us during crab catching, opossum (manicou) hunting, and turtle catching—and even for our fishermen who desired a well-lit massantow in the early morning after a hard night on the sea.

We were excited to leave home that night finally able to

flex our muscles and enjoy doing some manly things. We were not up to visiting some of the regular crab-catching spots, so we went to a couple other areas where we sighted only two crabs but were fortunate to catch them. Now two crabs were not enough, so we decided to journey all the way to the bottom of Ms. Irene's where we could catch some bigger crabs. I carried the caucus bag while Urias had the massantow blazing high above his head. The shoreline was always the shortest distance, so we continued nonchalantly through the still of the night. In my mind, I always viewed my brother Urias as a very coward chap, and for that reason I never felt totally protected in his presence.

One particular time while we were walking, I had a leery feeling and wanted to turn back, but I did not disclose it to him. We continued walking until we were just about to pass the last part of Basin beach. Then all of a sudden, the massantow fell and broke, and without delay Urias darted toward the shoreline. "I see somebody, I see somebody," he exclaimed softly, again and again. Immediately that triggered my nervous system, and big beads of sweat began running down my forehead. I had to make a split-second decision, so I started to follow him in quick pursuit with all the energy I had.

There was not enough time to think; I could not tell whether he had seen or heard something. I held the bag tightly and was able to close the gap between us. Our quest was simply to distance ourselves from the location of his sighting. We were approximately ninety yards away when we looked back and saw that the wick from the massantow was still burning, and the grass around it was on fire. I was not surprised; I'd had enough experience with my brother in the past to know that he could literally run off and leave anyone behind if he ever felt the least bit threatened.

Though we had been somewhat shaken, we still had a bit of courage left in us, so we decided to return to the area of his sighting. Some time had passed, and we were curious to look at the grass that was on fire. We walked the beach a few feet before converging on the blaze. There we found ourselves just a few feet from two men with bags walking toward the shed that I mentioned earlier. We froze there for a few seconds, and these seconds escalated into a minute or two. Suddenly, four more guys appeared walking by to a red dingy where they were offloading some merchandise. "These are faces we have seen before," I whispered under my breath. The sighting of these familiar faces allowed my beating heart to slow down, and somehow I was at peace with myself. Then unexpectedly, a bottle from one of those guys fell into the water. Urias grabbed it immediately and handed it to one of the men, but the bag-like box the man was carrying was so unwieldy that he could not receive it at the time. He returned a minute later and began to ask us, in a very friendly manner, our names and what we were doing alone in the dark of the night.

Eventually, I found myself helping to hold the dingy steady on the shore from the raving waves. Urias, on the other hand, was busy helping to tote those box-like bags to the shed. We ended up with a few dollars in our pockets and a new flashlight that we eventually used on our destiny to Ms. Irene's. We were so excited that we never discussed what might have been the contents of those bag-like boxes.

We were elated to use our well-earned flashlight to get to Ms. Irene's, where we could catch some big crabs. We took a cursory glance at the grass on fire, but it did not appear to be escalating into anything out of control, so we did not try to put it out. We left the site immediately for our journey to Ms. Irene's. Our crab-catching venture was more than successful; there would have been enough crabs for another half bag, but we had only one bag. Within an hour, we were on our way back home, with the legs and claws of the crabs protruding from the bag; that was rather uncomfortable against our bodies. We wanted to carry the bag on our backs, but we would have had to risk getting clawed if we were not careful. So we took turns carrying the bag all the way home. On reaching home, we put the contents of the laden bag into a drum. We had enough crabs to last us for approximately three weeks after we had given some to our grandmother Telina Roach and her best friend Rosanna; they both lived at Point Lookout, Clifton.

A few months later as the rainy season made its approach; grass and shrubs began to grow profusely on the newly cut road. Because of a lack of proper drainage, the unmanned water eroded the road so badly that vehicular transportation was no longer possible. Maintenance was never done on the road, especially the part that turned at a right angle from Basket all the way to the hill at Mr. Izolyn. This continual growth of trees and shrubs, as well as the improper drainage of water on this road, caused it to look like a forest in only a couple of years.

As quickly as these men had come, they disappeared. They left an unfinished road that turned to a track and later to a forest. The holding house or safe house used to house their dingy and the numerous box-like containers were left at the mercy of the weather. Looters later removed the galvanized roof and wooden door, but as the pictures show, this fortress was well built to provide service at a time when they needed it. It can be seen at the western end of Basin Beach. It still is far from conspicuous, as it lies hidden by the evergreen Manchineel trees that provide shade at the beach.

Looking at what transpired, one can only surmise that the intention of these folks was never to build a house on Fort Basin. The clearing of the site was to provide a proper lookout for their valued commodity that they had expected at that particular night. Many have seen this structure I am sure, but never knew when it was built there or why. The next time you visit Basin Beach, take with you a camera; you might be tempted to take a picture.

ABBOTT MANURE

Abbot Manure is a familiar name to the residents of Ashton Harbor, Campbell, and to the entire island. What is Abbott Manure? Is it just a conveniently manufactured name?

In 1975, the sheltered Bay of Chatham became extremely busy when a yacht laden with merchandise was eager to offload its contents to stay afloat and sail another day. That was what Mr. Phillip Mondazie Thomas said he was told by three white men who boarded his watch house and coerced him into providing storage for their valued cargo, "Abbott Manure."

Mr. Thomas was born in 1905, in the neighboring island of Dominica. Almost everyone in Union Island had an alias, and there was no exception with Mr. Thomas, He was known as Mr. Verrette. In fact, only a few people on the island had known his correct name. Mr. Verrette found love on Union Island and became the mate of one of our native daughters of Ashton Valley. Being a paid watchman at Chatham, he subsequently had to make that secluded part of the island his home. His function was to take care of two houses on that plot of land that was reputed to be owned by a foreigner named Mr. Ray.

The sun was swiftly making its way to the horizon when he was confronted by the group of white men who wanted to use his home as a storehouse for their cargo, "Abbott Manure. "Although he had been breathless when they confronted him, he still felt a sense of status in that he had been privileged to grant his bequeathed superiors a favor. Huge bales of fully packed manure were at his doorstep before he could accede to their demands. He directed them to the two houses that he had been watching over. His little shack was just too small for the bulk of merchandise he had before him. Hastily, the merchandise was packed tightly into some rooms of the two houses that he was looking over. Mr. Verrette was paid a small sum and cautioned in no uncertain term to keep what he knew out of the public's domain.

A still tongue was all that was needed to avert the dissemination of this information and avoid alerting the frail authority (police) on Union Island. Just as these white men had arrived without notice, they likewise disappeared almost instantaneously, but not before cautioning him again that they were going to be back pretty soon for their prized commodity. Mr. Verrette really thought it was plant food, and he was sure he had the privilege to use a bit of it. After all, he had a garden too, so he made use of some of the plant food. This resulted in a drastic turn of events; many are still confounded even until today.

"A still tongue keeps a wise head" is a meaningful verse in the book of Proverbs, but in general, it is more rhetorical than practical. Residents of Union Island believed in the mass dissemination of news—and any form of information, for that matter. If something were to happen at Point Lookout, Clifton, within a few minutes the entire island will be notified. In Union Island, it is customary that people tells their neighbors where they were going, even if they were to leave their homes for just a few minutes. "Nabe, I am going to Clifton to see Cousin Mabel; I hear she's not feeling well." And after that, one could be questioned at anytime in that community about the trip to Clifton and how Cousin Mabel was doing. In short, everyone communicated everything.

Mr. Verrette was no different. If he had been reticent when he first visited Union Island; he surely had succumbed to the rigorous demand of assimilation. No one holds a secret on Union Island; no one. Well...maybe a few, but Mr. Verrette was not one of those few; it was just a matter of time before a strong drink would have him talking.

Some weeks had passed since those folks from the yacht had visited his home at Chatham Bay, and he could not resist the temptation of talking to some old friends about what had mysteriously happened at his home. Mr. Verrette had a small boat, and he usually left his new home in Chatham to visit his former home at Valley to see some of his old friends. There he could reminisce, have a drink, laugh, and have a good time. He also did his grocery shopping there as well. One Sunday afternoon at a local rum shop, Mr. Verrette kept repeating in a haughty way, "I big," but no one knew what Mr. Verrette was talking about. He would command the shopkeeper to serve him and his friends beers and liquor, and then before the table was empty, he would call for another round. Without giving too much away in words, he would repeat the words, "I big." He felt burdened and obligated to share his news bulletin. He wanted to "spill his guts" as the saying goes. He was exhibiting lots of hints, but he wanted someone to literally dig it out of him. "I big," he shouted again as he poured himself a drink into a glass. Because he was under the influence of alcohol, it was clear that the appropriate scenario was created whereby he could relieve himself of his burden. That evening he spoke in depth about his affiliation with his newfound white friends and the bulk of plant food that he was left in charge of. Unfortunately, that was the beginning of the end; no one knew exactly what he was talking about, but soon everyone became eager to find out. A week later, he offered samples of the fine manure to his close friend and another friend in the Campbell area. Mistake! That is all that was needed for this product to get into the hands of a couple of savvy people who knew just enough to take advantage of the situation. The first invasion of the houses at Chatham began on a Sunday while Mr. Verrette was out at the Ashton Harbor having a good time with his so-called friends.

On that same Sunday afternoon, Urias, one my siblings was on his way to the pastures of Ms. Irene to get one of the milking cows. On his way, he was skylarking, picking seaside grapes, and taking his sweet time cruising along when he came up to the famous Divi-Divi tree that overlooks Basin Beach. At that location, he could clearly see everything on that beach all the way up to Palm Island. On Basin Beach was a small fishing boat with some of the local fishermen, and they were offloading huge, boxlike cargo. "There was one female inside of that boat whom I know very well, he said, she was very compassionate but cunning as a fox; I waved to her, but she never wave back." That woman, whom he described, has been deceased well over two decades ago. At the time, there was nothing that Urias could have made out of what he had seen except to think that it was just another case of contraband, which was the norm. In fact, every shopkeeper engaged in that form of trade. It was until a few weeks later that he learned what the shipment was really about. But by the time he had found out what had been happening on Union Island, everyone else had already been informed. Remember now, the island was very small, and news did get around quickly.

So where did these guys get the box-like bags that they were offloading? One key thing was missing. He did not see a huge boat anchored in the deep where this small boat would have gotten its cargo. But the bags sure reminded him of the ones we had seen many months earlier when we met those white folks on Basin beach while on our journey to catch crabs.

Now, returning to the subject of this episode: Where was Mr. Verrette while his house was being looted? He had already shared his secret while under the influence of alcohol, and that was just about the end of that, or so he thought. How careless can a man be in the distribution of something that does not belong to him—and worse yet, making himself a target at such a secluded area? The product that was deemed to be Abbott Manure was now in every nook and cranny in Union Island. This was a result of numerous timely raids on Mr. Verrette's home when he left Chatham Bay to visit his friends at Ashton Bay. Some took boats to Chatham Bay, took the goods, and journeyed directly to Basin Beach, where the goods were offloaded and transported via vehicles to their diverse locations. In addition, lots of young men went to Chatham Beach on foot. It was reputed that bales of this product were found in many remote areas of the bushes of Colon Campbell, where they were hidden and protected for safekeeping.

Almost immediately, it was discovered that "Abbott Manure" was really marijuana."Oh, drugs are on the land," was the cry of the righteously indignant. Yet it was reputed that this product could be found in every home. In the meantime, the protective authority on the mainland of St. Vincent received circumstantial information about the influx of this product on the island. This resulted in another form of influx—policemen whose physical presence was viewed by the people of Union Island as adventurous rather than investigative.

The deluge of marijuana on Union Island was a novelty not only to Mr. Verrette, an innocent citizen, but also to the majority of older folks. They literally had never seen a sample of this product in their entire lives and could not differentiate it from any regular bush or herb. And they knew nothing about its constructive or destructive use. However, the word was out that it had value and was rather expensive. Every adult male then tried to get possession of this illicit product to make some money. But as occurs in the world of business, when there is a large influx of any product on a market, it can force demand and supply out of balance, lowering its worth. And Union Island being so small was just an added disadvantage to the "wannabe" pusher. A few took to the sea to sell their freebies to other regional islands for whatever prices they could attain just to get the product off their hands. Then there were a minuscule few that was really savvy; they did make good of their trade. Meanwhile, the protective force was able to get possession of a large quantity of the ubiquitous marijuana that surfaced from time to time, but without making any physical arrests.

One afternoon at junior secondary school playground, the students were playing cricket, then suddenly, two policemen came out of the nearby police station with three large containers of marijuana. They emptied the containers, heaped the contents into one large bulk, and then lit it on fire while students were still playing their game. The students stopped the game immediately and circled the fire in curiosity; the scent escalated as the fire grew larger. That pungent scent caught the attention of the whole village, and soon many people began coming toward the burning pot. The officers tried to keep the students at bay from time to time, but there were just too many onlookers. Some older folks were disgruntled and were voicing their opinion on how wrong it was to burn drugs in front of students, but these officers did not respond. The dried herbs were completely burned in approximately one hour, and then the officers took a couple buckets of water and put the fire out.

Realizing that his properties had been fully relieved of the valued commodity, Abbott Manure, Mr. Verrette became mum and reclusive, and embarrassed that he could not trust anyone, even his best friend. He did not know who had stolen the manure and hence could not ascribe the blame to anyone in particular. His spirit was dampened, but he still had the will to live. He began to spend longer periods at his recluse in Chatham Bay. Unfortunately, loneliness would prompt him to take his small engine boat back to Ashton Harbor, where he would again exhibit his generosity by spending a few dollars and having a couple drinks with his so-called friends. It was the only form of recreation that he had, and he found solace in it. The two words that he had been using incessantly with authority (I big) were no more; it appeared as thought they had gone into seclusion.

After about eight months, all developments surrounding

Mr. Verrette had become "stale news." Most people thought it had all concluded and that those white folks would not return to Union Island any more.

One Sunday afternoon, after having a drink or two at a local rum shop at Ashton Harbor, Mr. Verrette left. The shop was rife with activity when suddenly a tall white man with blond hair and blue eyes showed up. In a calm voice, the gentleman asked about the whereabouts of Mr. Verrette, having been alerted of Mr. Verrette's weekly itinerary. The shop was instantly silent. The lanky fellow finally asked again in a calm voice, "Where is Verrette?" Hesitantly, they told him that they did not know who Mr. Verrette was. Reluctantly he left the shop without uttering another word and was never seen again.

What was quite amazing was that after Mr. Verrette had his fill with his friends, and as drunk as he often was, he would get into his boat all by himself, start up the engine, and head all the way back to his home in Chatham. And despite his state of drunken stupor, his friends never saw fit to accompany him to the lonely destination he called home. This he had done a number of times; his final trip was on a Sunday afternoon in the month of December. Many residents of Campbell can still remember seeing this little engine boat as it passed Frigate Rock on its way to Chatham Bay. It was the last time that I saw Mr. Verrette and his boat as he eagerly made his way beyond Queensbury Point into oblivion...permanent oblivion, that was.

One day later, Mr. Verrette's little engine boat was found at Long Rock, an area at Chatham Bay. It appeared as though the engine had been powering the boat continuously without direction until it ran out of fuel. As a result, the exterior of this unmanned craft was harshly battered and bruised. But there was no sign of Mr. Verrette; remains of foodstuffs were found inside of the boat when it was retrieved. The dwellings of this old man at Chatham Bay were quite intact, and there were no signs of foul play or a break-in.

Two days later, the old man's body was found floating some 200 meters off the shore of Chatham Bay, in the vicinity of Long Rock. His body was immediately towed to the Ashton Harbor later that evening, where it remained until the following day. He was buried early that day at the Ashton Cemetery, a burial ground that bordered the seashore. To date, no autopsy was conducted on the remains of Mr. Verrette's body. It was reputed that fish to some degree had eaten his body.

To this day, no one can be certain how Mr. Verrette spent the final minutes of his life, whether he met his doom at the fate of his own drunkenness or at the hands of a skillfully revengeful predator. Everyone seems to agree it was the latter.

Rumor had it that this mysterious yacht that approached Mr. Verrette at Chatham Bay had narrowly escaped the surveillance of a marine drug enforcement agent.

SUBSISTENCE FARMING

The lengthy dry season experienced annually in Union is the sole reason Unionites use water very sparingly. In short, water conservation is paramount on the island to prevent water shortage. There is not much difference between the conditions today and those of a century ago; Union Island has a semi-arid climate, and the island can be exceedingly dry during the relentless dry season that begins in the month of December and lasts throughout May. The island is disadvantaged in that it does not possess a rainforest or rivers like the mainland (St. Vincent) do; hence water conservation is integral to the life of the people. This is not exclusive to Union Island and the rest of the Grenadines Islands; it extends to the mainland of St. Vincent when there is an extremely dry year.

As mentioned before, in Union Island, there are no rivers, public desalination plants, or major reservoirs to provide, supply, and distribute water throughout the island to the people. Hence, the island remains devoid of water pipelines and may remain that way for another couple of generations. Unfortunately, the only source of clean drinking water is the water that has been conserved in cisterns and water tanks during the intermittent rainy season. The rainy season begins in the month of June and lasts through late November or December. Recent notions had it that a vibrant rainy season is contingent on Unionites successfully ingratiating themselves to the rain-god during the annual Maroon festival. Unfortunately, this perception is far removed from the truth and is facetious at best.

Unlike the mainland, St. Vincent, whose principal crops are bananas, plantains, breadfruits, sweet potatoes, and much more. The principal crops of Union Island are now corn and pigeon peas. For decades, corn and peas were grown extensively throughout the island but decreased immensely during the early eighties and nineties. Unfortunately, the level of cultivation has never returned to its previous form. Acres of land that were once cultivated with huge quantities of corn, pigeon peas, cassava, okras, potatoes, pumpkins, watermelons, and peanuts (ground nuts) now lie barren to the ever-present shrubs and some species of trees that are deemed nuisances to the vegetation.

Cotton was the principal crop that generated a substantial sum of money over the years when the landowners did not have to pay for its production. Cotton met its ultimate demise in the late 1960s–70s, but in reality the cotton industry was impacted negatively after the abolition of slavery in 1834. There were two types of cotton in the region; they were Marie Galante and Sea-Island Cotton. The latter supplanted the former because the plant was not as huge as its counterpart (Marie Galante) and was much more productive as well. Yet one of the impediments of Sea-Island Cotton crops was that they were more prone to worms than their cousin (Marie Galante). As a result, inspectors made sure that new plants replaced old plants annually. The main advantage of doing so was that the smaller plants made the cotton much more assessable during the period of harvesting. During its heyday, it was said that the cotton crop generated an average of about £250.000 per annum; this is quite a substantial amount of income, but it could be attained only under the auspices of chattel labor.

Several years after Charles Mulzac assumed command of the cotton industry, a cotton gin was introduced on the island. It aided in the cleaning of the product prior to export. This very useful machine supplanted manpower, a process whereby sharecroppers struggled to separate the multiple cottonseeds from the valuable fibers, which was used for fabrics. The ever-present seeds of this plant were useful for the production of cottonseed oil, a vegetable oil widely used for cooking. Its cholesterol content is very low compared to that of many edible oils. The foods fried with this oil maintain a long shelf life because of its antioxidant qualities; this was a plus when conservation was of concern during those earlier days.

Observing his father's declining condition, Richard Mulzac assumed command of the challenging cotton business. A few years later, he handed the responsibility to his son Irvin so that he could focus his attention on the large herd of cattle that they reared. He also conducted extensive marine trade in the region. Like Richard, Irvin was a shipwright by trade, a profession that he inherited from a family of boat builders. His extraordinary skill in boat caulking placed him on a pedestal way above everyone who caulks boats on the island. The cotton gin that he operated was located in the vicinity of the Sunny Grenadines Hotel, which was located above the home of Mrs. Adela James, a resident of Ashton Village. The steps of this ancient building are still visible today, many years after the building was razed.

In 1931, exactly one year after the death of Richard Mulzac, there was a mishap at the cotton gin. This sudden accident caused a young female worker to lose one of her arms. Dora Campbell of Ashton Village, a female in her late twenties, was employed at the Mulzac Cotton Gin. She was an excellent worker, in a position that Mr. Irvin Mulzac and his wife Rosalind of Barbados thought she had been well fitted to, and might even be irreplaceable. One morning while she was feeding the raw cotton through the spinning cylinder of the cotton gin, her left hand got caught in the teeth of the machine. Mr. Gifted Ramage, her coworker who was stationed at another part of the factory, heard her screams but misinterpreted the sound of her voice. He later saw the bloody discolored cotton and surmised that something drastic might have happened to the young lady. He tried to alert other workers of his finding, but unfortunately, the words of the stuttering young man were uncharacteristically vague and unclear. With no help available, the young mother's left arm was severed all the way up to her shoulder. She received medical attention later that day.

This young lady immediately assumed the name "One-hand Dora. "But the loss of her arm did not prohibit her from doing her daily chores or living a normal life, for she was still able to cook, wash, and use her garden hoe proficiently. The name "One-hand Dora" stuck with her for the rest of her life. She died in her sunset years in 1972.

Three decades after the injury at the gin, a continual decrease of cotton production on the island coupled with other commercial problems resulted in the permanent demise of the once lucrative cotton industry. Subsequently, the factory was rendered out of commission due to inactivity.

Now with corn and pigeon peas being the principal crops on the island, are they the staple of the natives' diet? Many may be inclined to say, "Was," but time will be the litmus test as this crop delves deeper into the twenty-first century. Up until the late 1980s, every family was engaged in the planting or sowing of seeds. Secondary crops such as cassava, okra, sorrel, pumpkin were also sown simultaneously.

The seeds or kernels of corn are sown in holes twelve inches wide by four inches deep that are approximately three feet apart. Six or seven seeds are then scattered into the dug holes and covered with soil. Pigeon peas, on the other hand, are planted in smaller holes about eight inches in diameter by four inches deep parallel to the corn. Four seeds of pigeon peas are scattered into these holes and covered with dirt. Then four or five days later, new plants emerge from the earth. The corn germinates a little faster; it is a member of the grass family. It is wise to soak the seed of both the corn and peas in water ahead of time to accelerate germination. The seedling at this stage takes minimal time to germinate. Two days and they are up out of the earth.

The seedlings of the pigeon peas take a little longer - emerging in another two days. The fresh seedlings are in their vulnerable stage and can easily fall victim to worms and the ever-present blackbirds. Every Unionite is familiar with the destructive nature of the ubiquitous blackbird. Children often hear their parents and older folks talk about how they were not allowed to attend school as often as they should because they had to stay at home to guard the seedlings against these notorious birds, whose proper name is the Carib Grackle. As small as the Tropical Mockingbird (Packer Chin-Chin), this blackbird of Union Island is notoriously destructive by nature. It cuts the shoot of the young germinating corn in its quest to gain access to the seeds under the earth. And it continues, incessantly cutting each young seedling from hole to hole and then scratching the earth for the seeds until it has its full. Then it flies away to a neighbor. That is why six or seven seeds are put into one hole with the expectation that one or two may fall victim to the blackbird or fail to germinate. Sometimes many corn-holes are void of corn because the blackbird is the first visitor. In many gardens, corn is replanted over and over because some holes may be short of two or three plants as a result of the blackbird's undoing. This is just one of the hurdles that the farmers of Union Island have endured to get the crop from one stage to another.

At one time, the scarecrow (Bwar-Bwar) was used to deter the blackbird from its incessant destruction on the cornfield, and it did work for quite some time. After a few weeks had passed, however, it appeared that those blackbirds had done their own observation and analysis and realized that these humanlike figures didn't move except when the wind blew. They began to land and defecate on them for good measure. As a result, the problem of the blackbird was back where it started and remained a permanent one for many years.

Everyone disliked the blackbird; young boys would set numerous traps to catch them alive.

Fortunately, the problem of the blackbird is no more. Is it because of the vast reduction of corn cultivation that was once practiced throughout the island? Or is it that the diet of the blackbird has evolved over a period of years? Whatever the reason, it is clear that some other type of food has replaced this bird's affinity for corn.

"Long ago, blackbirds were lethal enemy number one to every gardener, but they are almost domesticated these days. They land a few inches away from us, unconcerned about the presence of humans as they make their pursuit for the same cooked food that we eat." These were the words of Kenneth, a resident of Ashton as he explained the disparity between the blackbird of today and those of yesterday. "Long ago, they were hunted down into oblivion," Kenneth continued. "In fact, we used to set traps for them, and whenever one was caught, its feathers were drenched with kerosene and lit on fire, and it was allowed to fly to its instant doom."

During the heyday of the corn & peas crop of Union Island, no one was remorseful about the brutal death of a blackbird at the hands of a farmer. The children who were the watchdogs of the gardens sang this song.

Ay ba naughty blackbirds pass straight and go your way,

Mapu ripped ah Banta pick em up and say poo.

Ay ba naughty blackbirds Pass straight and go your way,

Long way for you to go, Mapu ripe ah Banta, time for ah-we go home.

Picture of the female Carib Grackle on a pigeon pea tree.

Children throughout the island sang this song in their gardens during the early hours of the morning to stave off the blackbird while it was most aggressive. They also had to be attentive during the late afternoon because these birds were not easily deterred. They actually thought that the black bird in some way understood the song that they sang and would eventually go away. Mapu, as mentioned in the song, is a small purple-black fruit that grows on an evergreen tree, the Mapu tree. It was a favorite fruit of the local birds, especially the blackbird.

Another significant problem related to the corn crop in Union Island was the infestation of worms. These worms, or caterpillars as they are called, feed greedily on the corn leaves before they make their long transformation into the pupae stage to complete their metamorphosis. So there were quite a few problems and challenges before the people could even get to the point of harvesting a drum (barrel) or two of corn and pigeon peas.

Corn took approximately three months from the time of sowing to harvesting. And although the plant didn't require much intensive care, corn and its immediate sibling, pigeon peas, had to weather the storm of challenges met by grazing animals. Cows, goats, sheep, and even pigs could not resist the temptation of a lush green cultivation. Animals caught inflicting damage on any plantation could be pounded (seized until the owner paid a ransom for the damage wreaked by his livestock). In most cases, these animals were returned to the owners without charge because people during those early years had a very strong sense of cohesiveness that transcended beyond monetary value; it was a condition that is almost nonexistent today, unfortunately. This was one of the strong values that existed decades ago.

During the time of corn harvesting, some are picked while the bulk remain on the plants to dry a couple of weeks. They are later harvested, and the corn stalks are carefully cut to make room for the pigeon peas to grow. The harvested corn is then placed on caucus bags or canvas and left out in the sun to dry while still on the cob. After two weeks of drying in the sun, the corn is manually removed from the cob (shelled) and placed on These same caucus bags or canvas to further dry in the sun; at this time, 80 percent of the liquid has been extracted through the sun's heat. By then, the entire drying process is completed, and the corn is then poured into huge steel drums for storage. Many local farmers take pride in growing huge amounts of corn—more than two drums. Farmers during the old days were truly dedicated to agriculture and would put in the labor and sacrifice to gain the best yield possible. At the end of a good corn season, every farmer would have enough corn to last beyond another year of harvesting. After one year in these huge barrels or drums, the corn was referred to as old corn. During such time, a new crop would again be harvested.

Corn had multiple uses. One major use was as feed for the poultry that was present at everyone's homes. Large amounts of these fowls are reared for poultry and fresh eggs. Chilli Bibbi, another product of corn, is a powered-like candy that is made from ground patch corn (popcorn). Sugar and spices are added to embellish its fine taste. This of course is every kid's delight.

Every home had two grain-mills; one for making cornmeal while the other is used for grinding the pre-dry corn for making green-corn dumpling. Cornmeal is used for making wangoo and wangoo pwah, which every native relished. The latter is a recipe in which pigeon peas are integrated into cornmeal to make a very delicious dish. This recipe for both dishes and other delicious dishes can be found in *The Stewart Cookbook of Union Island's Favorite Recipes.*

The women of Union Island are undoubtedly some of the best chefs in the region, second to none in local culinary art. Mrs. Eileen Stewart, Mrs. Jenny Charles, and many others have migrated to North America but attained their cooking skills directly or indirectly from Union Island and have kept the legacy alive. Having a dish of Pelau with locally grown pigeon peas from the kitchen of Mrs. Norma Thomas of Ashton Village will evoke a severe feeling of longing. A stranger served this dish may be tempted not to leave without having acquired the recipe. The sad truth here is not what is done, but how it is done, and indeed cooking in Union Island is done with passion. *The Stewart Cookbook of Union Island's Favorite Recipes*, dedicated to the late great William McDowell Stewart, the patriarch of the Stewart family of Union Island, is now available to all. Every Unionite should own a copy of this book; in fact, it should be in everyone's kitchen if they are adamant about keeping the legacy alive for their children and the children of their children.

Pigeon peas are another predominant crop on the island. This crop, like corn, assumed the position as chief crop from its ancestral predecessor, cotton. While these two crops may not be extinct on the island, it is believed that these crops will meet their demise in the near future. Sweet and bitter cassavas (yucca) are yet another crop that was home to Union Island. It made its way to the island as a crop to feed the slaves due to its rich content of carbohydrates. This gave the slaves the required energy to work hard and long hours on the plantation. Sweet and bitter cassavas are distinct in color; the stem and leaves of the sweet cassava have a pinkish color while the bitter is darkish green. The bitter cassava was used extensively by the local women to make farine and cassava bread even into the 1970s. Today, this practice is archaic. The women of Union Island were the rulers of the land, the homes, and the garden while the men were the rulers of the sea. The women of that day played an important role in the production and manufacturing of food.

Well then, what has contributed to such a massive decline in agricultural production in Union Island? Did the ancestors err in passing on the baton to the current generations such that it has significantly impacted the culture of the island? As mentioned before, the aversion to working the land, which has spiraled down through generations is a very important factor to look at carefully. Today's generations have willingly relinquished some essential building blocks particularly in agriculture. This entailed abandoning the hoes, cutlasses, and plows, and disassociating themselves from the laborious task that accompanies gardening. From their perspective, they have never experienced or witnessed the gains of the land translated into dollars and cents. Another important consideration is the ever-present force of technological transformation that youngsters are unwittingly swayed into. It is here to stay. And now, the big question, "The Exodus Factor," is it so consuming that masses of Unionites cannot resist its gravitational pull? Is it because of Union Island's size, coupled with its daunting semi-arid climate, a dearth of jobs, educational opportunities, and the legacy of governmental disenfranchisement that the island has inherited since the time of Charles Mulzac? These issues, and much more, must now be looked at objectively.

Natives will accede that subsistence farming is a thing of the past, for they are now inclined to frequent the stores and supermarkets for all of their staples. They regularly visit the neighboring island of Carriacou for staples that were present in their own backyards just a few decades ago. During the golden days, rain represented productivity, which rendered lots to eat, stock up, and sell. It was during that time that every household took up their garden hoes, cutlasses, forks, and rakes to till the land in preparation for farming.

◆◆◆□*Chapter Seven*

THE VESSELS

From the late nineteen century until the last quarter of the twentieth century, many vessels that were owned and operated by Unionites have circumnavigated the regional waters of the Caribbean: the Spartan, Ocean King, Lady Osprey, Wanderer, Wild Rover, Paragon, Priscilla, Pursuer, Providence, Katherine, Franklin D. R., Prince Louise, Utah, Radel, Lady Jestina, Lady Sylvania, United Kingdom, West Indian Eagle, Zena S., Olanda, Champion, Speedy Queen, Federal Queen, The Asco, Faith H., Adelta, Aloma, Yvonne Marie, F.S. Elizabeth, Sylvia E. M, Virginia, Flanders, Seamang, Angela, Kelvin & Clyde, and Armour Marie. The gold medal for the largest boat owned by any Unionite went to Mr. Augustus King Mitchell. That boat was The Triton (Aloma), which he purchased in St. Lucia.

Then there were the United Pilgrim and United Brothers, two vessels jointly owned and operated by three brothers: Gurry, Eastman, and Evan Stewarts (excellent shipwrights). The feat of partnership among brothers is nonexistent today, for the concept of collaboration is more likely to be met with these choice words: "A partnership is a leaky ship." A competitive, contentious spirit has replaced that strong feeling of cooperation of long ago. This new level of divisiveness or discord has contributed to the demise of many business ventures that would have benefitted Union Island greatly.

Many of the above-mentioned vessels have frequented the Gulf of Paria and the mouth of the Demerara River on a regular basis. Most of them were called Windjammers because they were seldom motorboats, and hence were operated by sail only. The men and patriarchs, effectively governed the island in a unique way, alleviated Union Island from many strains and challenges and have warded off the emergence of abject poverty and wants.

Many can now reminisce how the jetty of Clifton Harbor

was trafficked with commercial livelihood when these vessels made their way into the harbor after they had engaged in interisland trade. They returned laden with cargo through the hostile seas that engulf Jamaica, Trinidad, Cuba, Puerto Rico, Dominican Republic, Haiti, Barbados, and Grenada. These vessels were the lifeline, the aorta upon which the people of Union Island depended for oxygenated blood because the regional trading was important both commercially and as a food source.

Basic foodstuffs such as rice, sugar, flour, cooking oil, canned orange juices, powdered milk, and the like were imported from Trinidad regularly. They were sold, not just to the natives of Union Island but also to other nearby Grenadines' islands such as Canouan, Mayreau, and Carriacou. Clothes and regular household goods were obtained from this regional trading, primarily from the island of Trinidad where there was a wider array of manufacturing industries. During such time, St. Vincent, the mainland, was in its infancy in terms of manufacturing of clothing and similar commodities.

Long ago, the flour imported from Trinidad was bought in 100-lbs white canvas bags that were very sturdy. Locals made use not only of the contents of those bags but also of the fabric the bags were made of. They were used to make shirts and pants for children to attend school. And they were washed, thoroughly starched and ironed every week. A school child back then had but one uniform and was quite content with it.

On Union Island, local produce was exported to generate income. Exported commodities included tamarinds, sea-moss, crabs, corned fish, and Devi-Devi. The exported Devi-Devi was used in Trinidad for making soap or glue. Foodstuffs, textbooks, and other needed school supplies that were boxed and tied with yawn-rope (a type of rope) were bought in Trinidad and shipped back to Union. Portland cement, blocks, rebar (steel), lumber, nails, and screws constituted additional cargo that made its way to Union's hardware and shops.

Many of our local crafts sank, or in some cases ran aground, at nearby reefs. The last of these vessels was Speedy Queen, which was part owned by Mr. Mills Mc Intosh, the late Milford Mc Intosh, and Ifield Pope of Clifton. It is alleged that this vessel sank between the unfriendly waters of Trinidad and Grenada—"the Bocus," as it is locally called.

The *Speedy Queen* was built in 1964–65 at the harbor of Calliaqua, St. Vincent. After attaining all the information and expertise he desired, Mr. Mills McIntosh left the North Coast of Colliers Wood, England, in the London Borough of Merton, having determined how he wanted this craft to be built. "We needed the best lumber to build this ship," said Mr. Mills Mc Intosh, the mastermind of this whole venture. "At the end of the day, the consensus was to import from Guyana and Surinam all building material, chiefly the lumber that these countries are renowned for." He went to the town of Calliaqua, St. Vincent, where two local shipwrights nicknamed Mr. Gudgy, and Building Hucot took to the harbor to complete their new assignment.

This boat took exactly two years of painstaking time in the shipwright's yard of Calliaqua before it was ready for sea. Gudgy and Building Hucot were very committed and excellent at their craft, and they did deliver as promised, after two years of meticulous work. Upon completion of this arduous task, the bottom of the ship was cast with a special type of concrete for extra stability. Then two Rustan engines out of Lloyds, England, were installed, containing four cylinders each, and a gearbox of German origin, the Hurth. These engines gave the boat the kind of power needed to travel the rugged seas of Trinidad and Tobago, Guyana, Surinam, Venezuela, and the Windward Islands.

"Things were happening financially," said Mr. Mills. "We had constant revenue that was showing significant signs of prosperity. I captained the vessel for its entire life except that one voyage on October 3, 1970, when it went missing. Things do happen at sea," Mr. Mills, whispered dejectedly. "My heart is telling me that those poor chaps were asleep when disaster met them that Saturday night." On that vessel were the other part owners: Milford McIntosh and Ifield Pope, the husband of Princess Pope. Seventeen other passengers and sailors were a part of the voyage. They all perished at sea.

Earlier I made note of some personalities that have grazed the soil of Union Island. Their contributions and legacies have left an impact on the island. But I would be remiss if I did not mention the true cornerstone and bedrock of this little island, Mr. Augustus King Mitchell. He was the owner of the most vessels in Union Island during the 50's and 60's. His empire extended into numerous small business, from hotels to real estate. His formative years at the Anglican Church School were indicative of his aspiration not to settle calmly into the status quo of "just getting by, or coping. "It was clear at an early age that he had entrepreneurship written all over his psyche. And like Captain Hugh Mulzac, his hunger to excel could not be satisfied within the confines of the Grenadines waters. He wanted more than what was proffered to him and was bent on attaining every ounce of what he aspired to.

LIVES LOST AT SEA

Even before the 1940s, numerous Unionites lost their lives to the unforgiving waters of the St. Vincent and the Grenadines, Grenada and Trinidad, Martinique, and so on.

Thursday, June 19, 1989, is unquestionably a night to remember. It affected me both positively and negatively, but by and large, there is something worthwhile to be learned from such tragedy. At that time, I was living at my brother's home in Washington DC. That evening, I was at home taking care of some personal things; Earlrick and his wife, Lucille had left for church. A few hours earlier, I was sitting in the living room looking at TV for approximately twenty-five minutes. Nothing seemed to grab my attention, so I kept changing channels rapidly. I was just about to put down the remote when suddenly a strange feeling came over me. My body began to shake uncontrollably. I looked at one of the windows facing the street, and immediately a commanding voice inside of me ordered me down onto the carpet. There I remained for another several minutes as my body continued its shiver. Then, almost instantly, a burst of energy inundated me. I rose without delay as though nothing had happened. Little did I know that my brother Urias was breathing his last breath at sea during those few moments while my body was unable to contain itself.

Back in Trinidad, my mom, Sheila, had an alarming dream one week prior to Urias' tragic death. She was at the Bethesda Gospel Hall Church, Port of Spain, where she attended the Sunday service. She fell into a brief nod and dreamed about the roaring of the sea and its many waters. Among the waters, she saw knives and other sharp-edged weapons as they moved violently to and fro. "It was a slumber that sapped the energy out of me." She said, "I woke up gasping for breath; I was very tired."

Two days later I received a call from a very close friend out of Trinidad named Gracie Ford, who said a boat of seven men, all from Canouan except my brother, Urias, had left Union

Island laden with beverages for Canouan but sadly did not get to its destination. It was an extremely sad time for us as a family. This was a tragedy that we had to deal with nonetheless, though it did not compare to the countless lives lost at sea through negligence and bravado.

Over the years, the native fishermen or cargo boat owners of Union Island did not wear lifejackets. This practice of nonchalance was handed down from one generation to another. From every corner of Union Island, the shoreline has been available to every resident: "It's just a hop, a skip and a jump away" as we say colloquially. And for that reason, 99.9 percent of the people knew how to swim. That may have hindered their sense of a need for precautionary measures to avert the dangers at sea. Here are the names of some residents who have lost their lives at sea then, and in recent years.

Mr. Ben Hypolite and his little son Simon, Jobe Alexander, Albert Lewis and wife Elizabeth, Elnora McTair (child of the late David McTair), Howe Wilson, Ms. Flora Douglas and Mrs. Newly Harvey (the first wife of the late Tyrell Harvey and mother of Nimrod Harvey) all perished in the seemingly benign waters of Union Island and the sister island, Carriacou. This sailboat of Union Island left the jetty of Hillsborough, Carriacou, on a late Monday afternoon on its voyage back to Union Island. It never got to its destination. It is believed that they were between these two islands when a sudden windstorm or twister got the better of them. The captain, Ben Hypolite, along with the other eight passengers, did not stand a chance; the boat was not fortified with lifejackets or any other reliable facilities that could have saved lives. They disappeared almost instantaneously.

One young man from Ashton Village claimed to have seen the little craft moments before its unfortunate disappearance. He did not notify anyone until the following day. This lad was the son of a trafficker from St. Vincent named Ms. Locus. She once sold her produce, or ground provisions, at the well-known Meldon shop of Ashton Village. Mr. James Cox originally owned this shop and later sold it to Mr. Meldon John of Campbell. The chap later distanced himself from Union Island as residents expressed their displeasure at him for withholding such valuable information. Had they known that the boat was seen that afternoon, help would have been sent out in search of survivors.

Another small boat from Union Island almost encountered the same fate. This boat left the calm waters of Hillsborough, Carriacou, where many residents go to visit doctors or shop. They had lots of groceries, ground provisions, and fruits. The captain and his boatload of passengers were well on their way home, but before they arrived to the deeper blue waters, a sudden gust of wind capsized the little craft. The bulk of their groceries, along with the ground provisions and numerous bananas, floated everywhere. They held on tenaciously to the semi-submerged craft, and fortunately, fishermen in the area saw the incident and immediately rescued them. Two individuals who experienced this close call were the late Mama James and Ms. Wilhelmina Adams. The latter was well known throughout the island as "Dune. "It was reputed that one woman, despite the severity of the situation, found it necessary to have her fill of the bananas that were floating around while awaiting rescue. Nevertheless, all lives were preserved, and they were able to get the boat back into working condition almost immediately. The boat and the entire crew got to Union Island later that day.

February 18, 1966

At about 9:00 P.M Friday February 18th, 1966, a small boat laden with conch left the quiet harbor of Ashton on a journey to the commercial port of St. Georges, Grenada. The captain, Mr. Theopolis Longdon, traveled with a crew of four, namely Lovell Eustacious Scrubb, Stanley Davis (Tall Boy), Cecil Longdon, and a minor named Tyler Thomas. All were quite excited on their trip. It appeared to be a smooth, comfortable voyage as they sailed through the exceptionally calm waters. They had long since passed the little island of Carriacou and by now had completed over 70 percent of their journey. A discussion started about Mr. Nicky (Tin Dada), a seaman on a previous trip to Grenada, who was reported to have been relieved of his entire purse of $60. Members of the crew began talking about this and were probing to determine whether anyone on this crew might have been responsible for that crime; the discussion turned into an argument.

One member of the crew, Stanley Davis, felt he was disrespected when some members indicated that he was responsible for the deed. In disgust, Tall Boy stood up and pointed his hands in the air and shouted, "If I took the money, this boat ain't reaching Grenada." Instantly, his words came to reality.

"Everyone's eyes were fixated on Tall Boy's hands in the air, and as he took his hands down, the boat became submerged with the cargo of conch. Miraculously his words had become reality, Tyler Thomas explained, it was around twelve midnight; I don't know what had happened. That was something else, and it still bothers me; every so often when I remember it. Everyone was in the water just like that. Lovell's feet were on my shoulders and he pushed me right under the water, causing me to scramble about. I still remember the sweater I had on. The tide was very, very strong and moving up in an easterly direction. It swept us up immediately. From the beginning, Tall Boy started to complain about cramps in his feet. I heard him moving in the distance. I did not hear anyone else except Theopolis, so I started to swim until I caught up with him. Boy, we kept swimming together for a while, and suddenly Theopolis said to me that he didn't think he could make it. I was shocked to hear that, so I said to Theopolis, 'Pray Theopolis, just Pray.' Then I started to sing 'Rock of Ages cleft for me, let me hide myself in thee.' that was all I could do: swim and sing; that was my only hope."

Tyler Thomas, the youngest of the crew, was the son of Mrs. Norma and William Thomas. He swam with the old man thirty-one years his senior and took a proactive stance in motivating his older compatriot never to give up. Without any land visible in the dark, Tyler had a sense of what direction they should swim. He encouraged his elder as they swam blindly through the hostile current. Five hours later, they saw land. It was early in the morning, way before the sun came up from the horizon, and there lay a cay that they later learned was Big La Than. The tide by then had changed direction, but it was so strong that it prohibited them from reaching land almost until midday.

"Well we reached Big La Than and rested on the sand for a while, but there was no form of help," Tyler said. "We looked around and saw another small island with smoke coming out of its bushes; the island was Little La Than. We decided to swim to that island to get some help. Boy it took us another 30 minutes to get there, but the smoke was still a distance from us."

The curious sixteen-year-old then shouted for help. Realizing that help was in the distance, they both climbed down the rocks to the other side where they would be able to discover the source of the smoke. They went to explore and sighted a couple of campers.

Excited that help was available he told the two men of the horrendous situation that they had endured. The campers served them breakfast. They started eating, but because the older man had drunk a lot of seawater while swimming, he vomited profusely. They finished their breakfast, rested for a short while, and then decided to climb the rocks in search of their fellow crewmembers. They got to the other side of the small island and immediately Tyler saw his tired friend Cecil (Sagga) very close to a rock, just about to climb to safety. In excitement, he said to Theopolis, "Look Sagga." The older man hastily looked and saw his son as Tyler cautioned him not to call him. But the elated dad couldn't contain himself upon seeing his beloved son on the cusp of safety. He shouted "Cecil!" and immediately Cecil turned his head in the direction of his father's voice. Instantly a strong wave washed him under the water. Both men stood for a while waiting for him to resurface, but he never did and was never seen again. They wept bitterly.

The campers later took Theopolis and Tyler to the port of Sauteurs, north of Grenada. There they attained much-needed help, and the news was later broadcast to Union Island via St. Vincent. The men were later transported to Granville, another small town of Grenada. They spent the night there, and early the next day they boarded a boat that safely transported them to the port of Hillsborough, Carriacou. In Carriacou, a small boat from Union Island titled Zag, captained by the late Cecil Regis (Differs), was patiently awaiting the two men. Cecil weighed anchor, and off they went to Ashton Harbor, where 90 percent of the residents awaited their arrival.

At about 2:30 p.m., the little craft reached Ashton's Harbor, where a thousand plus happy residents mobbed them. "It was like a melee that afternoon; everyone was happy to meet and greet us." Tyler said, "Unionites really turned out that afternoon, Josiah; they did I felt a sense of oneness. I felt loved."

Lost on that voyage were Cecil Longdon, the son of Jessita and Theopolis Longdon, and Stanley Davis, the husband of Mrs. Faithful Ackie. Also lost was Lovell Eustacious Scrubb, the son of Pablo and Rosa Scrubb. Theopolis longdon, now deceased, was the husband of the late Harriet Longdon and father of Winston Longdon. Tyler Thomas is the only surviving member of the crew that left for Grenada on that late Friday afternoon some forty-six years ago.

After witnessing the disappearance of his son on February 19, 1966, Theopolis Longdon's heart remained heavy with grief and pain for the rest of his life. Theopolis was buried on March 20, 1995.

June 25, 1985

Nelson John and Sherwin Wilson, two young teenagers lost their lives on a small boat (Top Gun) between the waters of Grenada and Carriacou. They were returning home after a successful trip to Grenada and were never seen again. No physical evidence was ever found. It is believed by many that the severe rough waters of this region swamped this crew. Nelson John was the son of Jessie and Thomas Polson (Uncle Tom) while Sherwin Wilson was the son of Emris Wilson.

August 5, 1983

A crew of four from Clifton Harbor—Glenroy Alexander, Julian Adams (Huggins), Kenroy Alexander, and Johnathon Snagg (Ranking lost their lives at sea on a journey from Martinique back to Union Island. This boat, *Wandering Star*, was captained by Kenroy Alexander and was on its weekly voyage back from selling fish and shrimp and then buying nonperishable goods to be sold locally in Union island.

It is believed that they were met by a severe storm on a dark, rainy morning, and the boat overturned. This conjecture was reputed by some based on a few unusual occurrences that preceded its disappearance. Holden Regis, the captain of the vessel *Sweet Memories*, was also engaged in the same maritime venture. He had left Martinique one day earlier but did not encounter any abnormality on the water. "The water was nothing out of the ordinary. It is not that it was entirely calm, but nothing to lose sleep over." And even though we believe they became victims of the capricious weather and the rant of an unrepentant sea, it remains a solemn mystery. Many question whether foul play occurred. But even if that was the case, we still muse pose these questions: Did they have lifejackets? Did they have a radio whereby they could have communicated for help on such a regretful night? These are some of the unanswered questions that haunt us whenever we have losses at sea, especially the precious lives of our loved ones. Below are some of the events that led up to the disappearance of *Wandering Star.*

One day after Wandering Star had docked in the port of Fort de France, Martinique, the crew of five observed an unusually pungent scent coming from the deck of the boat. The scent was so obnoxious that it was impossible for them to remain on the craft. But everyone wondered where the scent came from; no one had an answer. The crew questioned whether a liquid had been intentionally poured in their absence to dissuade them from returning to the boat. But the question is—by whom? With the help of friends, the crew worked feverishly to rid the boat of its intolerable odor, and they did. Ready to return home again, they pulled anchor and set sail on the voyage back to Union Island. A couple hundred meters off the harbor, another unusual occurrence, grabbed the attention of the crew. This time it was the rudder of the boat that was showing signs of failure. Sighting problems ahead, the captain turned the boat around and headed back into the harbor of Fort de France. There the problem was addressed, and early the next morning the boat was ready to sail again. One member of the crew, Reynold Mills (Tamboo), was rather disgruntled and chose to remain ashore rather than sail the following morning with his compatriots. It turned out to be a prudent decision. It was the last time the boat was seen. Reynold later returned to Union Island on Good Fortune, a boat that was owned by his brother, Newton Alexander.

June 19, 1989

On June 19, 1989, Urias Stewart, and a crew of six young men, all from the island of Canouan—Trevor, Dannie, Chris, Curtis, Boyie, and Byron—sailed from Carriacou, where they had bought beers and other strong drinks earlier that day. They stop on Union Island on their way to Canouan. Urias could not resist the opportunity to travel with them he wanted to attend a party that night in Canouan. Urias was excited to celebrate with his on this sister island. His friend at the jetty of Union Island tried to discourage him from traveling late that evening, but Urias could not be dissuaded. It was already dark in Union Island. Urias was the last to board the boat. They left quietly that evening and were never seen again.

Earlier that year, there was litigation against Urias by a foreigner and that the foreigner was dissatisfied with the outcome of the lawsuit. Some think that may have sparked some sort of reprise from the foreigner who knew that Urias was about to travel on the unguarded waters; the foreigner seized the opportunity for revenge.

Did these six young men meet their end because of Urias' presence on that little craft? Did they? This is some food for thought.

A minuscule few believed that the little boat, laden above its capacity with liquor, was easily swamped in the somewhat choppy waters between the islands of Mayreau and Canouan.

March 15, 1991

Denzil Stewart's demise was another tragic death that could have been avoided. This gentleman died in the same ostensibly shallow waters that appeared to be only a stone's throw between Union Island and her sister Isle Carriacou. The festive atmosphere was approaching, and everyone was rather uneasy as they eagerly awaited the famed Easterval Celebration. Rumors had it that Denzil Stewart and his friend Junior Coy were totally drunk yet had still embarked on a journey to Carriacou regardless.

Residents later learned that the above was inaccurate. This is what had happened as was reported by Junior Coyaka (Ground-E).

It was approximately 12:30 A.M. on Thursday, March 15, 1991, at the Ashton Harbor. These two gentlemen may have had a drink or two, which was quite normal. Denzil expressed in no uncertain terms that he wanted to go to Carriacou and would like Coy to take him there immediately. Coy, however, was not happy to leave Union Island at that time of the night and tried to dissuade his friend. Denzil was not taking no for an answer, so Coy's position seemed to fall upon deaf ears. To keep his friend happy, Coy acquiesced. Both men got into Top Gun, the little boat that was owned by his brother Jacob Coy (Lassie). They started the engine, and off they went into the dark of the night.

They had barely reached the midpoint of their journey when the outboard engine that they depended on to take them quickly to the port of Hillsborough suddenly shut off. They tried for approximately fifteen minutes to get the engine back in working condition but to no avail. Their patience was swiftly diminishing with every unsuccessful effort they made. Realizing that the little boat was drifting quickly, Junior decided to swim to Carriacou to get help, for its lights appeared not too far away. Denzil decided to stay on the small craft in hopes that help would be available shortly. Quietly, Junior got into the water and off he went swimming towards the lights of Carriacou. But two minutes had not yet passed when he heard Denzil's voice shouting, "Ground-E, wait for me, wait for me."

Ground-E did just that and swam hastily towards him. Without lifejackets, both Denzil men swam together for approximately 30 minutes supporting each other amid the raging waters. They were quickly succumbing to exhaustion because they had not rested the preceding day. Denzil, the bigger of the two, began to show signs of helplessness but persevered at a slower rate. Seeing that his friend Denzil was in despair, Junior asked him to hold onto his shoulder in an effort to alleviate the strain of his tiring arms. The heavy boots on Denzil's feet were a gross disadvantage; it made swimming more difficult.

"In the beginning, the lights from Carriacou appeared to be close, but the more I swam, the less improvement I saw," Junior Coy recollected. "I was so tired that I could barely keep my head up. The weight was keeping me down, and Denzil appeared to be drinking water." Relieving Denzil from his shoulder, the fight for survival came down to a war against the relentless water. "I was a little ahead while Denzil with gallant effort swam slowly behind."

Junior became emotional "All I know is the sea Josiah, it is all that I know." As the light the morning brightened, he lost sight of Denzil. Cold, tired, and exhausted, Junior remained hopeful that help would come to him even if he had to make it to the shores of Carriacou swimming, which was still far away. His hope became a reality at about 9:00 A.M. when Jasper H., a small engine boat that was owned by the late Festus Hutchinson of Ashton Harbor rescued him. Denzil, on the other hand, was nowhere to be found. Neither was Top Gun, the little boat belonging to his younger brother.

January 24, 1997

On Friday, January 24, 1997, Captain Ledger Alcide (54), his son Otway Alcide (21) of Union Island, Bertram Daniel (65) of Mayreau, Yvonne's son (23) of Union Island, and Dallo (35) of Lower Questelle, St. Vincent, all perished at sea. These entrepreneurs engaging in commercial trade with the French island of St. Maarten left the sheltered harbor of Kingstown during the wee hours of the morning, heading toward the harbors of Phillipsburg and Marigot. The craft never made it to its destination and was never seen again. Although not much can be said in conjecture of this boat, enough time has passed to bring us to a consensus on this one. Mr. Ledger left behind his wife, Millicent Alcide (Liz), and children, namely Curtis, Yolanda (Pinky), Joy, David, Raymond, and Lavern.

It is believed that this boat sank in very rough waters, where help was unattainable. Mr. Ledger Alcide, who was well known as Dick Richards, was the hardest-working young entrepreneur on Union Island. Dick had recently sold a vessel and had migrated to the United States of America, where he lived for a short time. Dick's livelihood was etched in the Caribbean, and he loved the Sea with a passion. He later left America and reverted to what he knew best: marine life. Well, he wasted no time, and again he was the owner of another vessel that he bought. This time he named this new craft Flying Lobster.

Armed with a crew of four (mentioned above), Dick immediately immersed himself into a friendly trade relationship with the cosmopolitan island of St. Maarten. His cargo was ground provision, plantain, bananas, and a wide variety of young plants that he sold to a market that was tailor-made for him. On his return to the islands, he would bring with him refrigerators, TVs, VCRs, and so on to be sold to the locals of Union Island. He also brought back cooking oil in large quantities, knowing that there was a local market for that product as well.

After eight months of inter-island trade, Dick knew his way around this new frontier. As a result, business appeared to be doing fine, and he and his crew took advantage of every opportunity that presented itself. One week earlier, they had been scheduled to make a trip to St. Maarten, but because of the inclement weather in the region, they were forced to remain on land until the weather condition subsided. On January 24, they eventually pulled anchor, and off they went into a calmer sea to the great beyond, never to be heard or seen again.

February 14, 1997.

Coincidentally disaster struck twice that year, and on the same day of the week to boot. Friday, February 14, 1997, is another date that Unionites can commemorate with the burning of candles. This time the culprit was the roving water of St. Vincent and the Grenadines. Rupert Polson, (Jah-Pot), as he was amicably called, left the port of Kingstown late one Saturday evening, between 4 to 5 P.M., heading for Ashton Harbor. Two other young chaps—Rocker and David—accompanied him; they both were from the mainland, St. Vincent. Another sailor on his way to St. Vincent claimed to have seen the boat as they both traveled in opposite directions. The time had passed when these three young lads should have been back. Relatives and friends became more concerned with each passing hour. With their eyes affixed on the once-narrow passageway that separates Frigate Rock from Union, everyone hoped for a propitious sighting, but unfortunately without success. The early morning swiftly turned into noon, and noon made its way to another sundown. The optimism that had been exhibited twenty-four hours earlier, suddenly evaporated. A strange feeling of sadness arrived and lingered, as everyone was forced to accept defeat. The island had lost another battle to this aged enemy and friend, the sea. Once again, Union Island wept.

December 21, 1968

One of the most gruesome accidents in the waters of the Grenadines was the sinking of the passenger/cargo boat, Federal Queen. Although this accident happened some forty-plus years ago, it is still fresh in the minds of Vincentians, especially the families whose loved ones perished at sea.

The late William Stewart of Ashton Valley, Union Island, owned Federal Queen. On December 21, 1968, this small vessel weighed anchor and set sail for the mainland of St. Vincent. As it left the harbor of Clifton, Union Island, onlookers quickly lost sight of this little craft as she disappeared into the darkness of the night.

William Toast, as he was locally called, had a boat load of

people who were from the mainland but had been employed in the Grenadines returning to their homes for Christmas. Rumor had it that the boat was full above its legal capacity. It had approximately eighty-six people onboard, and some people had reluctantly come off the boat a few moments before it left. Of the many people who came off the craft, two notable persons were the late Jonah Stewart and the aforementioned Dick Richards, who met his death twenty-nine years later on a commercial voyage to St. Maarten. Yet it is alleged that one mother literally pushed her son onto the loaded craft to ensure that he did not miss his opportunity to travel. Oh what a mistake that was. Nevertheless everyone knew that she had meant well.

All seemed well when the vessel left the choppy waters of Union Island, but it immediately became an uphill battle for the captain and the crew as the craft entered the deeper waters. The island of Mayreau immediately became visible as small spots of light were seen in the not-too-far distance. These spots represented kerosene lamps—the only source of light besides flashlights that were battery operated. But as the island of Mayreau instantly became visible, after another thirty minutes, it was totally out of sight. They cruised by Mayreau and were in the vicinity of Canouan as they continued into the darkness of the night. The shadow of Canouan, too, was out of sight when they trespassed into the unfriendly waters that led to the Bocus. The Bocus, which is sometimes called Pateau, is the roughest part of the sea in the Grenadines. The boat was far from this seemingly volcanic-like wave when a gush of water swept across it. The large crew moved frantically from one direction to another, and down the boat went. One survivor indicated that while he was sitting, nodding on himself, he felt his bottom drenched in water, and a few minutes later the boat went down with everyone."

The sea was now flooded with disoriented people. They began to panic in the dark of the night. A lighthouse in the distance caught their attention, and immediately they began swimming toward it. Unfortunately, that was away from land and safety. Some, however, did have a sense of direction and swam where they thought the island of Canouan was. Susan, the lone female survivor, was a resident of Georgetown and was among the first to swim to the island of Canouan. She once lived with Mrs. Lucita and Robert Joseph (Arthur Gill) of Union Island. William (Toast) Stewart, the captain, Alston Ramage, and Jeffers Jones (T-Nana) of Union Island also made it safely to the island of Canouan. Ken, another native of the mainland, was also among the few survivors. Though they knew well how to swim to land, they were far from being prepared for such a Herculean task.

Forty-plus lives were lost on that early morning of December 22, the majority from the mainland. One who stands out was a resident of Georgetown by the name of Envy Pitt. Two others from the mainland are John Mike and Clifford John. The deaths from Union Island were Ottley Jones, the son of Mrs. Rosalyn Jones; Alfred Gellizeau aka (Din-Din), the son of Priscilla Gellizeau; and finally Norris Dickson, a friend of the late Stella Badnock. It is reputed that a young woman was found alive in the water the following day. She was rescued but later died of dehydration and exhaustion.

A wave of sadness inundated Union Island that morning when the news was dispersed. That day the wind refused to blow on a day that relatively cloudy. Residents spoke in very low tones as if they were whispering so that the next-door neighbor would not hear. The truth is, everyone felt the pain of his or her collective loss in a country that was far more community-minded than it is today.

Over the years, many more have lost their lives at sea. Listed here are names of a few: Godwin Wilson, Medford Wilson (former judge of Grenada), Reynold Gellizeau aka (La beau), Hayden Hutchinson, Terrence Joseph, Edmond John, Peterson Cox, Tommy Coy, Lyndon Stewart, and Mathew Alexander.

"Marine preparedness" can and should be enforced in St. Vincent & the Grenadines by the appropriate ministry to safeguard lives, or in some cases to save the youngsters from themselves.

HURRICANE JANET

It is reputed that Hurricane Janet may have been one of the most destructive hurricanes that grazed the soil of Union Island. It shared huge similarities with the "Windward Island Hurricane of 1898" yet was not as bad as the Great Hurricane of 1831, whose impact on the region was unprecedented. Janet's destruction on the islands of St. Vincent and Barbados was also astronomical, not to mention the effect on the rest of the Caribbean Islands that lay in the path of this redoubtable force of nature. Many older folks are familiar with this calypso sang by the late Lord Christo of Grenada in the year 1955; for people of the Caribbean, this song will conjure up memories of such time.

Ay Janet, ah beg yo hard, Jar...net, not Trinidad
Ay Janet, ah beg yo hard, Jar...net do not Trinidad

Yo blow down the whole ah Grenada,

Same-way the Barbadian suffer.

And every day we read the evening news,

enough to make ah man jump out he shoes

Janet hide in the mountain, Janet lick-down a million building.

Janet sister was Kathy, Janet blow way the whole ah Miami.

On September 22, this category 3 hurricane, packing a force of 115 miles per hour, slammed into the region, causing extensive damage to the islands of Barbados, Grenada, St. Vincent and the Grenadines, and St. Lucia. It is reputed that the island of Grenada suffered more damage than the other islands. Known for its vast production of nutmeg and other spices, Grenada suffered a loss of approximately 75 percent of its nutmeg plants to this raging wind. The coastal areas of St. Lucia were devastated by this Atlantic hurricane. St. Vincent was literally leveled, which resulted in a setback of its chief agricultural product, bananas. The region suffered upward of 160 deaths at the hands of this natural disaster. Some claimed that the number quietly surpassed 500 deaths. Fortunately, only two lives were reported lost in Union Island.

Prior to the hurricane, leaflets were haphazardly dropped from an airplane that hovered over Union Island. This was meant to alert the residents of the imminent danger and that no one should leave the shores of Union Island on a boat. Although many hastily received the information, some had no idea that leaflets were dispersed. One small boat from Clifton had left Union Island a little while before this information was disseminated. They had left for Palm Island, a hunting ground of crabs and farmland for planting sand-potatoes. Residents also harvested salt there.

On that boat to Palm Island, was one of my late great-aunts, Jenney Roache. She was also the sister of my grandmother Telina Roache (Tan Tillix) of Clifton. The late Mrs. Margaret Ovid and a few other people were said to be on that adventurous trip, as well. They reached Palm Island safely, unaware, and then after almost 20 minutes on the little island, they had to abandon their task and seek shelter under the same raft that had just brought them safely across the water. They turned their little boat upside down against the wind, leaving enough room for each one of them to crawl under to safety. They were packed like sardines in a can, but that was the least of their concerns; their primary objective was to remain alive.

The whistling sound of the sand coupled with the incoming rain made it rather impossible for them to sleep during that eventful night. I had the opportunity to listen to Aunty Janie on a rainy afternoon as she talked of Hurricane Janet. "It was like a sand-storm that refused to end," Aunty Janie whispered softly to me. She placed her hands over her ears as though she heard the horrified sound of the sand all again, and reacted to what had transpired some twenty-three years earlier. Then suddenly a huge smile surfaced on her previously melancholy face. "We used to get a lot of turtle eggs, whelks, and conch in Prune, even paddocks we used to reap by the bags. Those days were good days," she said, chuckling. "I could never forget that beautiful island." She shook her head and walked slowly into her bedroom.

On Union Island, the seemingly sheltered harbor of Clifton was not as fortuitous for the Seamang; a vessel owned by King Mitchell (entrepreneur) was also smashed to ruins. The Lady Sylvania, another vessel that was owned by the late Peter and

Samuel Wilson was also moored in the harbor. Meanwhile, on land, numerous residents lost their thatches at the hands of this vicious storm. Even today, many residents talk about events that transpired during Janet's reign of terror. "It was one of the most memorable disasters that Unionites have experienced within the last sixty years." One resident said. "One thing that stands out most conspicuously about the wrath of Janet was Mr. McKay John's wooden house being physically moved from its location and deposited, intact, some three hundred yards away." She continued. Ironically, that place of inertia was among the countless tombstones of the Ashton Cemetery. One native of Canouan who once lived in Union Island mentioned that her son was born during the time of Hurricane Janet; she just could not remember the exact date and year.

Ms. Mappish, the mother of the most acclaimed tailor of Union Island, Mr. McNeal Cox, had quite a bit to say about her misfortune at the hands of Janet. She was nicknamed Mappish, which was short for Ma Patient. Only older folks will remember that her name was Patient. This Ashton resident had lived opposite the building that was used as the dispensary that was once home to the late but well-known shopkeepers Joseph Alves (Daddy Alves) and his wife Edith.

Remembering this hurricane, Mappish stretched her hands outward, pointing at her huge plum tree that fell, then shouted: "It's only by the grace of God why I still live today." Her younger sister, Ce Julie, had her say as well as she spoke passionately, as though it had happened only a couple of days ago. "You see all across here was water, the whole place flood!"

Still further inland in Ashton village, countless thatches lay feebly signifying the presence of this unprecedented reign of terror in the island. In Clifton, the situation was identical; some were fortunate enough to lose only their roofs. With the strength that Hurricane Janet possessed, they were at God's mercy. Isabella Roach (mentioned earlier) was among the countless residents that lost their wattle and daub houses. She found refuge at her son's house. His name was Johnathon.

As the horrendous sound of the raging wind preceded the presence of Hurricane Janet, one parent out of fear, placed her babies and toddlers into cabinets. She thought that the cabinets Were the safest place for her young ones. Fear inundates every parent on hearing the bending sound of the galvanized roofs that reacted like paper.

Other hurricanes of note were Hurricane Hugo of 1980, Hurricane Lenny of 1999, and Hurricane Tomas of 2010, whose presence was felt mainly in St. Vincent and St. Lucia. Nevertheless, none had been as memorable as Janet, whose presence brought fear to the minds and hearts of Unionites..

◆◆◆□*Chapter Eight*

ALL FOOLS' DAY

Though this book may chronicle a few challenging times of my life, there were indeed many times of joy and humor as well as intriguing events that will definitely raise a few eyebrows. Many who once lived in Union Island may be able to empathize with me; your misery or woes, bliss or glee may escalate into a hearty well-deserved laughter, or even tears after many, many years of suppressed memories. But before I get to what I really want you to know, let me share with you what my good friend had to say. She shared the "Then and Now" opinion as she touched on the subject of April 1st All Fools Day:

"April 1st, known as 'All Fools Day,' was an age-old tradition from the days of colonialism and may have started sometime during the late sixteenth century. The Caribbean later embraced this particular day from the British settlers and passionately made it their own.

"April 1st in the Caribbean was a day that everyone would try to remember because it could prove costly and embarrassing if you were oblivious when that day rolled around. On April fool's Day, the young and old alike played mischiefs on their friends, neighbors, and other villagers. These mischiefs were designed to fool the individual with the intent of having a good laugh when discovered hours or days later for that matter.

"Sadly, it is clear that the disappearance of many of our treasured cultures and traditions has resulted from the modernization of our societies. That once significant day of the year now comes and goes without the slightest bit of acknowledgement. With the advent of the cell phone, iPod and other electronic devices, the possibility of playing a well-organized prank on another person is simply a thing of the past.

Sadly, the best description is to refer to it as archaic. Today, even the youngest among us would question why they should have to take a note to another person—a district away—when "they can easily make a phone call or send a text.

"Suffice it to say that modernization, like everything else, has its advantages and disadvantages. One of the disadvantages is the loss of our rich heritage—the customs and traditions of the ancestors on Union Island. Inability to manage the cultural transition because of evolution has resulted in the loss of the baby and the bathtub as it is said proverbially.

"Generation X and Y will never know the true meaning of April Fool's Day in Union Island because they have not experienced the creative ways that our friends and neighbors once played those tricks on us. They will never hear the loud bursts of laughter across the street when the trick was discovered or see the embarrassment on the faces of those who were tricked. Gone are those good old days!"

Yes, my friend is quite on point with her keen observation; I could not agree more. So now, let us focus a bit on one of my personal experiences on Union Island.

I was eight years old in 1970. I was sent to do some shopping at Mr. Robert Wilson's shop, located approximately half a mile from my home at Bottom Campbell. Groceries during those early days encompassed rice, sugar, flour, cooking oil, butter, baking powder, black pepper, and other basic necessities and condiments for everyday use. Unfortunately for me, that day was All Fool's Day.

I did most of my shopping at Mr. Robert's shop. His nickname was "Toe Joe," but on that day, Toe Joe did not have any cooking oil, so my next bet was Mr. Wilton Wilson's shop, or so I thought, and there the old fiasco began. Everyone knew him as "Wash Brain," a nickname that he had inherited earlier in his life; I have no knowledge of its origin. But I can take solace in referring to him as "Brain Wash" a couple of times here.

Well, in Mr. Brain Wash's shop, I got one bottle of cooking oil, paid for it and was just about to leave when he said, "Boy can you deliver this note to Mr. uh... Ambo for me?" I nodded affirmatively as he grabbed an old cement bag, tore off a piece of paper, scribble a few words, and then wrapped the paper in an unkempt manner and handed it to me. "Don't open this paper; just give it to Ambo. You could leave your groceries here until you come back."

I was harmless as a dove and obedient as a rented mule, so there was no way that I could have made any excuse or refused to go; that was not in the keeping with the culture. I took the rumpled brown paper, but before I could leave the shop, he warned me, "Do not give it to Teacher Mary, okay?" I replied yes in a very soft voice and took off to deliver it to Mr. Ambo, who was another shopkeeper.

Now, Teacher Mary was Mr. Ambo's wife, and surely Mr. Wilton did not want that paper to get into her hands because she was a mother herself and might be more ethical and compassionate, and that could have subverted his clandestine plans. "Good morning Mr. Ambo," I bellowed as I walked quietly into his shop. I handed him the note and informed him of its origin. He unwrapped the paper and stared at me for a few seconds, and then a cunning smile emanated from his previously straight face. My eyes were now fixated on him as he summoned me not to leave just yet. I did not have the slightest idea of what was going on or what to make of the note or of his now hefty laughter. Soon after that, he too tore a piece of brown paper from a cement bag, jotted down a few lines, and told me to deliver his note to Mr. Hudson Mulzac. "Deliver this to Cayenne Waste for me quickly; don't open it, okay" And off I went to a sprint to get this note to its destination as quickly as I can. It is presumed that Mr. Hudson Mulzac (another shopkeeper) got his nickname, Cayenne Waist, from the city of Cayenne, the capital of French Guiana.

"Good morning, Mr. Hudson," I recited, breathing heavily when I walked into his shop. Mr. Hudson was fully attired. His shirt was in his pants, and his pants were well above his waistline. That morning I thought he was using his belly to keep his pants up because his pants appeared to be a bit too big. He took the note and read it without exhibiting a smile; he was as serious as a beast as he stared at me from head to toe. One of his eyes was a bit off, and at one moment I could not determine whether he was staring at me or at something nearby. I was quite shaken, looking at his pants well above his waistline. "Who you boy, who your parents?" he asked. "Mr. Garfield's son," I replied, still a bit shaken. "You could go by Cleve Mulrain for me?" He forcefully asked.

I was in a daze by that time, totally taken aback by his question because Mr. Mulrain lived almost halfway between Clifton and Ashton, and that wasn't anything less than 45 minutes of brisk walking for my small feet. But, on the other hand, I started to think reward. If he sent me that far, obviously he would reward me monetarily—though I did not have the boldness to say it. At that moment, I could hardly stand upright in front of that man without trembling slightly.

But fortunately, he never forced the issue, so I did not have to walk such a length in the hot sun. Honestly, I believed that he was cold-hearted enough that, on my return, he would not have the faintest idea that I could have been thirsty after such a long walk, much less give me 25 cents. So I was exempted from going to Mr. Mulrain's residence, and I thought he would tell me to go home.

Instead, Mr. Hudson—or Cayenne Waist, as he was called—went to the back and got a clean piece of brown paper on which he scribbled something. "You went to Russell yet? What about Meldon?"

I replied that Mr. Meldon's shop was closed, but refrained from sending me to Mr. Russell's. Even now I wonder why he did not send me to Mr. Russell's shop, for he did not appear compassionate in any form or fashion. He pondered in displeasure and then handed me the note, "Take this back to Mr. Ambo for me."

So again I was on my way to Mr. Ambo's shop to deliver Mr. Hudson's brown paper note, but before I could get inside Mr. Ambo's shop, he again burst into laughter as he looked at my worried face and folded palm. I began to laugh too, for I was happy to see him laugh without restraint; his laughter was healthy and pure. That is the kind of laughter that I refer to as contagious and therapeutic, in retrospect. He took out his pen, wrote something on that same paper, and then whispered, "Take this back to Cayenne Waist just one more time, just one more time."

Now it had been a while since I had left home, and if Mr.

Robert's shop was the only shop I had visited, I should have been back home almost twenty minutes ago. So I knew that my parents had to be wondering why it was taking me so long. But how could I say no to an adult? I was concerned about returning to Mr. Hudson's shop with that brown paper, for I did not know what to expect of that man. He was as serious as a bull and looked so wild-eyed when he stared at me. I sometimes wondered if something was wrong with one of his eyes. I later learned that it was just a front that he was putting up to ward off uncontrollable folly among kids.

Mr. Hudson stretched out his hand to receive the brown paper once again, and then he proceeded to the back of his shop, his face bearing a slight smirk. "O God, not again," I muttered under the breath, but this man was adamant that I should be sent to yet another location. "You went by Jonah yet?" he asked me in a bold commanding voice, as though I should have been sent there a long time ago. "No," I replied, and out came the brown paper once again. "Take this to Jonah; walk straight." I acquiesced immediately.

I nodded and set off to Mr. Jonah's shop with yet another folded brown paper. It did not take me two minutes to get to Brother Jonah's shop, for he lived very close to the Gospel Hall Church and was an elder of that church as well. I was happy to be there because my friend and cousin Curtis Stewart was his son, and we had gotten along well since childhood—and to make things better, we were classmates as well. Brother Jonah immediately took the paper, opened it on the counter of his shop, read it to himself, looked at me for almost half of a minute, and then said to me with a smile, "Boy, go and meet your mother." It was only at that moment that I suspected that something was out of the ordinary, yet my innocence and naivety still would not allow me to understand fully what was taking place.

A customer stepped into the shop during the time he was exhorting me to go home to meet my mother, and immediately his attention turned toward her as he left his note unattended on the counter. Then suddenly the brown paper fell to the floor, and as I bend to fetch it I saw a couple of words that read: "FURTHER ALONG."

I took up the brown paper immediately and though no one was paying me any attention, but Mr. Jonah stretched out his hand to receive it, and I obliged. That day I felt totally embarrassed and uncomfortable, walking all the way back to collect my groceries. I kept my face straight ahead and walked quietly to Mr. Wilton's shop to get my groceries. I met his wife, whom we usually call Mom or Ms. Look-Sin. She handed me my groceries, and off I went all the way back to Campbell, where I took a verbal whipping for spending excess time up the village. I did not tell my parents that I had been sent out to deliver some notes. Yet I never figured out what the complementary words on that brown piece of paper were. Although this had a negative impact on me for many years, I treated this incident with personal care, and like other things that have transpired in my presence, I did not view them as issues to be shared it with anyone. But in my later years, I surmised that the preceding words on that paper may have read: "Send that fool a little..."

Can this or similar prank be done today with this current generation? You better believe otherwise. I am already hearing the answer. *Hells No!*

AN OLD YEAR'S NIGHT COOKOUT

It was Friday night, December 31, 1971. Three youngsters were eager to put the final pieces together on a cookout that they had planned a week earlier. Four other members, who were involved, provided the pots, dishes, rice, cooking oil, butter, sugar, and other condiments to cook a huge pot of Pelau that night. The only missing ingredient was the meat, which they had no intention of buying. The three chaps had suggested that they would have one of Mr. McKay's biggest roosters as soon as he left his home early that night for a walk up the village. Mr. McKay was an old farmer who lived very close to the road at Campbell Village. In his garden were a wide variety of fruits and vegetables. As kids, it was always a boon to pass his way; one could always count on getting a handful of peanuts, a slice of watermelon, or even a roasted coconut bake—a specialty of Union Island.

Many folks were afraid of him because he gave the impression that he could do a lot of supernatural things. And to make matters worse, he was living close to a calabash tree, which is reputed to be home of the zombie. The calabash tree (Boulie) was also located close to the street, and all of his chickens slept on that tree. These young chaps had already planned how they were going to catch the birds and they were going to get them before the clock struck 12:00 midnight for fear of zombies. The three youngsters—Garnett, Urias, and Stephen— decided that Garnett would climb to the top of the tree, catch the bird, and hand it to Stephen, who would be a few feet below. Urias, who was to stand at the base of the tree, was supposed to be the lookout, as well as the final individual to receive the roosters.

The three waited for McKay to leave his home, watching from Adrian Simmons' (neighbor) garden. Within minutes, the old man with his permanent limp was in the vicinity of Mr. Meldon's House. (Mr. Meldon lived a couple hundred yards away from Mr. McKay house.) The boys were safe now and had no intention of wasting a minute. Garnett, being lanky and agile, had climbed the tree in a matter of seconds and was closely followed by Stephen. Quietly, he grabbed one of the biggest birds and held its head tightly so that it could not make a sound. He immediately handed it to Stephen who further muted the bird before it got to Urias, who placed it into his bag. Sighting another huge fowl nearby, Garnett decided to take advantage of the opportunity and have a second. He handed it to Stephen, and they both descended quietly from the huge Boulie tree. Everything seemed to be going fine thus far.

The three young men quickly headed for the village, unnoticed by any of the neighbors. They then joined the other four members of the crew and decided to cook their food under a Boulie tree located above Mr. Gifted Wilson's house. With two flambeaus ablaze, everyone went to work. They plucked the two fowl, cut up the meat, and had it seasoned in a short period of time. It was about 11:00 P.M. when Stephen placed the pot on a three-stoned fire that was fueled by wood for energy. Every so often, passersby would stop to take a glance at the crowd of youngsters, who were busy being chefs. They were really having a good time.

Finally, the cooking came to a close. The smell of the Pelau was all over the area. All, but one of the members of the crew was eager to enjoy the fruits of their labor. While six youngsters, namely Stephen, Garnett, Terrence, Junior, Felix, and Henry, all sat down to eat, Sylvan refused; he was not satisfied with the way they had attained the meat.

I ain't eating because I don't want no fowl to crow in my belly," he said. The other chaps tried to cajole him to eat some food with them, but he was unyielding. "No fowl ain't crowing in my belly," he said again and again. He remained adamant to not even put a spoonful of the food into his mouth. Meanwhile, four members had finished eating and, still hungry, they went back for seconds of this delicious food. The food was now down to the bottom of the pot, and Stephen began scraping the last bit (Bun-Bun). Seeing that the Pelau was about to be finished, Sylvan became uneasy that he might not get a taste of the food. He held on to the pot and bellowed, "I go eat some ah the Bun-Bun; I don't want no chicken, just give me some ah de Bun-Bun, that's all."

Sylvan took the pot, scraped the remainder of the food,

and quickly devoured it. Everyone was basically filled except Sylvan. By that time, it was well past 2:00 A.M., and the crew of seven was having a great time. They remained under the tree for another two hours chatting and laughing, and were later accompanied by other youngsters who came on the scene to hangout.

The following day was New Year's Day. It was a very quiet day, and it went by quickly. Sunday was yet another quiet day, a regular church day, and that, too, went by quickly, with lots of youngsters attending their respective church.

On Monday morning, Stephen woke up very early and left his home to attend to his animals at Ms. Irene's. When he reached Mr. McKay John's house, the old man greeted him. "Ah Stephen, I miss two ah meh biggest cock fowl. Do you know anything about that?"

"True, Mr. John? That is real wickedness; I don't know anything about that, but that is real wickedness. That is real wickedness."

The savvy old man stepped closer to Stephen and asked, "You sure?" Stephen had thought that McKay would just ask him the question and leave it at that, but he was wrong. Feeling a bit nervous, Stephen was just about to leave when McKay said to him, "Anyway, whoever took my f@#*$% fowl has nine more days to live."

Stephen panicked upon hearing those words, and his heart quickened. Feeling fearful that he was going to die in nine days' time, Stephen stared at the old man for almost a minute and then whispered, "It was n-n-not me Mr. John, not me." Then he sadly left for his journey to Ms. Irene's.

Stephen hurriedly attended to his animals at Ms. Irene's without uttering a word to anyone he met. On his return, he quietly walked by McKay's house as though he did not know the old man. He immediately visited each one of his friends who had been part of the old year's night cookout, telling them that Mr. McKay had missed his fowls and that they had only nine more days to live. They were all worried; no one wanted to speak on that subject, fearing that they had messed with the wrong person No one seemed to be as concerned as Stephen and Sylvan.

"I don't think I will die because I did not eat any fowl; just the Bun-Bun," Sylvan said sadly.

"McKay say everybody go dead, everybody," Stephen replied. "We only have nine days left." The youngsters really needed help but did not know what to do, and they could not tell their parents of this ordeal because their backsides would have paid the cost. However, others began to sense that something was wrong with these young men because they were uncharacteristically quiet.

While at home that afternoon, Stephen sat for a while and pondered where he could get help. Then suddenly, he came up with an idea."I am going to visit Porcho (Mrs. Pricilla John). I think she know something about Obeah," he said softly to himself. Porcho was an old lady who lived opposite Ashton's Cemetery. "I think she could help me out." Within ten minutes, he was at the old woman's house.

"Good evening, Ms. Porcho," he greeted her.
"Good evening, son," she replied.

But before she could utter another word, he again said to her, "Ms. Porcho, I have a complaint to make. Mr. McKay says we have nine days to live."

"Nine days!" she echoed as Stephen hesitantly described in detail what they had done. "Boy, I don't think Sido (Stephen's mother) will like to hear that," she replied. "Boy who and you do that?" she questioned the nervous lad. He answered again with tears in his eyes. "Anyway, don't pay that no mind. Don't bother with McKay John. Nothing going to happen to you." She said. Well, that surely did not appease the troubled youngster, for he had just revealed in detail to the old lady what had transpired without receiving solace. "O right, Stephen, tell Siderlyn good night for me," said the old lady. "Okay, Ms. Porcho," he replied and left immediately.

Still dissatisfied, Stephen decided that he must get some help, and the only way he could get that help was through an old person. His other target was Daddy Mac (McCauley), an old fisherman from Carriacou whom he assumed might know his way around the compartment of superstition. He wasted no time revealing what had happened on that Old Year's night and mentioned all his accomplices, constantly reminding Daddy Mac that they had only nine days to live and that he must do something about it. Daddy Mac sat for a while and then laughed uncontrollably, wiping his teary eyes. The old man replied, "I don't think anything going to happen to you, but to be on the safe side, go under the Boulie tree where you cook the food and pray early each morning for nine days before the sun come up, okay All, all-yo." The old man again burst out in laughter and shook his head, amused. "So we wouldn't dead?" Stephen asked pitifully. "No," said the old man, and the lad left quietly.

Stephen was very contented to hear Daddy Mac's remedy; it was the first time all day that he felt at ease. The young lad immediately got the information to all of his friends and told them what they had to do to keep from dying within the next nine days. Unfortunately, anxiety got the better of him that night, and he was unable to sleep soundly.

Early Tuesday morning before six o' clock, the group of seven teenagers gathered under the Boulie Tree to start their first morning of prayer. Sylvan, realizing that he had been given another opportunity to live, took the state of affairs very seriously and brought with him a bell that he rang during the prayers. The other six members made use of their turns by praying meaningfully.

Later that morning, Terrence was on his way to Ms. Irene's and was greeted by Mr. McKay. "Terry, you in it, too!" the old man shouted. "No, Mr. McKay," Terrence replied, "I did not steal the fowl, but I eat some of the food. Yo cud forgive me, please?" he begged the old man pitifully.

Mr. McKay assured him that he would forgive him. On hearing that, Terrence begged the old man to forgive his cousin, who was also part of the plot, but Mr. McKay refused."No one else," he yelled. Although Terrence left feeling somewhat relieved, his relief did not prevent him from joining the crew under the Boulie tree to pray for the remaining days. They did it consecutively until the ninth day, and after no one had died, they were so remorseful that they all decided to do an extra three days.

CARNIVAL

The annual festive Easter season of early April is called Easterval, a combination of the word Easter and Festival. This season is drenched with myriad activities that encompass a Carnivalesque atmosphere. This attracts mass regional attention as well as residents of Europe and the Americas. Lots of people find their way back home for a full week or two of thorough enjoyment, entertainment, and play. During the earlier years, the annual carnival festivity was very artistic and cultural. It encompassed many bands with elaborate costumes that were skillfully displayed in the streets of Ashton and Clifton. Today, Jouvert begins very early in the morning as masqueraders dance in the streets to music that is played loudly on trucks. This "jump up" as we call it, starts at the basketball court, travels to Cross Road, Bordeaux, and on to Richmond Beach, where it ends.

For the carnival of yesteryear, all the costume bands would make their way to the Magistrate House at Clifton Hill. There they would perform at their best, exhibit their artistic skills and prowess, and subsequently be judged. Calypso competition was another activity of note. Young men and women of Union were very competitive for each year's calypso crown.

The atmosphere then was thick with excitement as residents crowded the streets in droves, eager to be a part of this annual celebration. Many can still remember the 1969 carnival when the street of Ashton was alive with the melodious sound of Trinidad & Tobago's "Road March Queen" Calypso Rose. Everyone was gleeful as they sang along to her song, "Fire, Fire in me Wire, Wire."

Carnival of yesterday dates back to more than eight decades ago, for that atmosphere was rife with numerous activities. The History Mass of Union Island was phenomenal; every onlooker's eyes were glued to these characters. The historical rendition of European history and speeches was

173

performed by older men dressed in elaborate kilt-like costumes, coupled with adornments that resembled those of a knight. They danced with an extremely long whip while intentionally projecting a mean-spirited appearance. Valuable characters such as all of the deceased—Ernest McTair, Claude Ambrose, James Stewart and his brother Henry Stewart, Peter Alexander, and the flamboyant Willie Edwards (the grandfather of Mrs. Merle Ackie) were all integral players of this artistic legacy. These key players in this once noteworthy History Mass of Union Island. The generations of today have lost interest and do not exhibit the same level of skill. The badge of honor once held by these players, whose profound knowledge of British history was unrivaled, is now archaic, for want of a better word.

Traditionally, the History Masses of Ashton and Clifton had to exhibit some form of make-believe rivalry among each other before they could make a pact among themselves. The site of this eventful gathering was Ce Courtney Bridge. You may ask, where is Ce Courtney Bridge? It's the same bridge that lies some seventy feet east of Cross Road in Ashton, which is now called the Dry-River Bridge. Ce Courtney Bridge attained its name from a native of Barbados named Mrs. Courtney Wilson. She was the grandmother of the late Augustine Cox, who has lived in that area for quite a while. So this point was where the two factions of the History Masses of Union Island would meet. The Clifton faction needed permission to cross Ce Courtney Bridge so the Ashton faction would engage them with numerous questions of European origin, taunting with their whips. Satisfactory responses usually resulted in an immediate pact and free passage over the bridge. An unsatisfactory response might result in a gesture-like whipping. In reality, this gesture was more a custom and formality than an authentic rivalry.

Everyone descended on Cross Road Junction (Green Corner) and around the Small School area, which was the center of this mass gathering and all other carnival activities. The Cross Road location was home to the popular Allan Scrubb, the grandfather of Mrs. Icena Wilson. Bah Allan, as he was popularly called, once had a shop exactly in the location that his great-grandson Kendall Wilson now occupies.

Many of these History Masses could approach any onlooker and demand money. The late Henry Stewart was famous for his two-line rendition: "Hezekiah give me meh Cora,

Hezekiah give me meh Cora." No one seemed to understand what he meant as he shouted loudly while brandishing his huge whip. The victim would become scared and reach into his pocket to dispense the pound, shilling, pence, or hapenny (whatever he had); he then would hand it over to the masked man (Henry) who would quickly take his fee and retreat quietly to sort out another victim.

The pound, shilling, pence, and hapenny were the monetary units that were used back then. The smallest unit, the hapenny, was worth half of a penny. They all were a part of the British monetary system still used in the Caribbean more than half a century ago. These coins have since been replaced by the Eastern Caribbean dollar, quarter, nickel, dime, and penny.

So yes, carnival was practically a whole day affair that encompassed numerous activities. Older folks can remember the late Cornelius Jones of Canouan Island, the father of Reginald Jones of Clifton. Cornelius was well known for his colorful Indian attire; he participated in the Indian Mass annually, with singing and dancing that depicted the East Indian culture. The East Indian culture became pervasive in the Caribbean after Indians from India were brought to Trinidad and Guyana as indentured servants. We can see clearly that all of these attributes that were interpolated into this eventful gala did have their rightful place.

The numerous activities associated with the annual Easterval gala resurrect the feeling of homesickness each year in the hearts and minds of nationals living in the Diaspora. Returning home to a slower lifestyle, every visitor tends to let his or her guard down just to relax and take it easy. The white sandy beaches are readily available, and no one knows these beaches better than a returning native. They are ready to assume ownership of the island that they have left decades ago without fully acknowledging the changes that have occurred. The conch, fresh fish, crabs, goat, and locally grown chicken are accepted and savored with joyful readiness. The corn-fish is relished; the roast corn, green-corn dumplings, wangoo and okras, sea moss, and a host of local delicacies are treasured like never before.

The Easterval celebration is indeed a time to shake a leg. A returning native won't be hesitant to do so; he or she is always in the thick and thin of all activities on the roster. Though there's not much nightlife in Union Island, in the evening, visitors amble everywhere in the street. Everyone knows each other, remember? So a feeling of cohesiveness enables everyone to feel at home once again. You are never a stranger there, for there is always someone who can clearly identify your bloodline and speak profoundly of your ancestors. "Boy you is ah Stroad; I don't know which side of the family you from, but I know you is ah Stroad." (Stroad is a local name used in Union Island that refers to the family name Stewart. Older folks today still used that name regularly).

Basketball completions, Queen Show, and parties make up the night's activities while boat racing (Regatta) and other sporting activities are done during the daytime.

Lennox Charles, a Unionite now living in Europe, revived the Steel Pan in Union Island during the early 1970s. As a result, the band was able to compete against other steel band orchestras in St. Vincent during Carnival festival. Lennox also introduced basketball to Union Island during that same period.

Union Island is definitely the place to be during the precious month of April each year. It is a month that is rivaled by no other time of the year; even the famed Christmas holiday is pale in comparison.

◆◆◆□*Chapter Nine*

CONSERVATION & WATER USAGE

The absence of rivers coupled with the severe dry season has caused the natives to use water very sparingly almost all year round. More than a century ago, numerous ponds and wells were dug to conserve large quantities of water. These wells, sometimes called waterholes, were located (a) at the Anglican Church, (b) next to Gospel Hall Church (c) at the sand hole next to the United Friendly Society, (d) Chatham Well, at Chatham Bay, and (e) Campbell well, at Bottom Campbell. The latter is less than eighty years old. Unfortunately, there have never been wells at Clifton, even until recently. During the early to the middle part of the twentieth century, many residents at Clifton had their personal ponds that they also referred to as waterholes. Most of these ponds were located at their homes. The owners of some of these ponds were Isabella Roache, Ms. Victoria Hypolite, May-May Hutchinson, John Snagg, and Ce Mammy; others had ponds located at Belmont and one at Top Hill, Clifton.

Some of the more significant ponds of Union Island were Pappy Son waterhole near Colon Campbell, John Stewart (Papa) waterhole, Basket Pond (Basin), Downson Pond, Rapid (Rapeet) Pond, Mulrain waterhole, and (the largest of them all) the well-known Lincoln Pond, which is located at Richmond. Residents call it Lenkin.

The wells and ponds were the location where clothes were washed. They took their huge bundles of laundry, along with wooden tubs, washboards (jerking boards), blue soap, and corncobs—to do extensive washing by hand. Washing by hand was the only means of taking care of the laundry. The cob of the corn was locally called "corn stick" and was used widely as a scrubbing brush. In this case, the cob was utilized for scrubbing clothes, especially jeans—or dungarees as they were called then.

Most people preferred to use the ponds and wells on Thursdays and Fridays for this purpose. On site, their clothes were washed and sometimes partially dried to reduce the weight before they took them home. At the homes, the clothes were hung on lines with wooden clothespins, where they would thoroughly dry later. Lincoln Pond was by far the best and most preferred pond on Union Island, even though Basket Pond (Basin) may have been the largest. Lincoln Pond had a spring, and hence when most ponds were dried up during the severe dry seasons, water was still available at Lincoln Pond. For that reason, most washers could be found there on both days of the week. The water there was very clean and drinkable; it did not have a taint of saline content.

Below is a picture of a typical well in Union Island; this one is located at Campbell, and was used for many years for washing clothes and feeding livestock.

Campbell Well served the residents for many years. The periphery of this well needs masonry work.

It is well over seventy years since water reservoirs were built in Union Island. The challenge of water shortage had to be addressed, and the reservoirs immediately aided the residents, who had to contend with the dearth of supply they experienced annually. There are two of these facilities. The larger is situated in Ashton Village, a few hundred meters above the Adventist Church. This provides water for the nearby Ashton community.

The chief recipients are those without huge concrete cisterns to conserve their catch of water during the evanescent rainy season. The other is located at the east of the island. This Clifton reservoir obviously is not as big as the aforementioned Ashton repository, but it serves the Clifton residents. Some dry seasons can be severe. The scarcity of wells, coupled with the abandonment and extinction of water holes, has given Clifton residents no alternative but to depend on transported water from St. Vincent. This water is then taken by trucks and sold to residents who made requests. In the eastern end of Clifton Harbor, a desalination plant is situated. This plant provides an adequate and efficient amount of water for those commercial enterprises, hotels, and guesthouses that are tethered to the beaches. This makes the water shortage a non-issue to tourists and visitors, even in the heart of the dry season.

The water situation is still a major challenge to residents, but is not exclusive to Union Island, for the rest of the Grenadine Islands encounter the same plight of water shortage annually. They had hope that the governmental authorities in St. Vincent would have addressed this condition a long time ago.

In the eyes of many residents, Union Island has never been treated fairly by the state of St. Vincent. As a result, Unionites openly expressed their desire to be governed by the neighboring island of Grenada at the turn of the 20th century. Unfortunately, Grenada declined base on the financial responsibility that accompany this task. Moreover, it is interesting to note that such level of neglect by the state of St. Vincent was not recent but aged-old.

Samuel V. Morse, a commanding engineer who visited Union Island on July 22, 1778, found the lack of water rather daunting. He was appalled by its scarcity and the health condition of the slaves. On the other hand, the Europeans used rainwater, which they conserved in earthen jars and well-built cisterns.

Dom Carlos Verbeke, a Benedictine priest, was also appalled by the condition that he observed in 1928. He described the grave shortage of water on these islands by indicating that there was scarcely anything to drink. He went on to say that the people had to scoop water from mud-filled ponds and that the island was devoid of grass to feed livestock. Nevertheless, he was overwhelmed by the people's desire and will to overcome such impoverished state. .

On Tuesday June 11th, 1891, an American doctor by the name of H. N. Nichols visited the island. He was a specialist in Yaws, (a highly infectious disease that affects the skin and bones, but is extremely easy to treat). This disease is similar to the aforementioned leprosy (Hansen disease) written earlier about some ailing residents that were placed at Frigate Island. On arrival, Dr. Nichols was astounded and felt compassion for the people whom he observed were very poor and totally neglected by the Government of St. Vincent, who only adds to their woes. He said that these residents were not benefiting from the state in any way, shape or form because they were not given anything. Not even the roads were upkeep; hence he was astounded that these good people did not drive them off on their arrival. He also learned that there were no concerns by the state for the wellbeing of residents who died indiscriminately when ill. This is primarily because doctors were not available to address their needs and concerns. He further indicated that when the tax collector comes around many residents took to sea with their little crafts to escape that burden. Those that could not leave the confines of this improvised rock had to pay by the skin of their teeth. They paid from the money they barely earned through inter-island trade to Barbados and Carriacou.

This form of disenfranchisement and neglect of basic needs and services had been perpetuated on the people of Union Island even unto the 1970's. What make matter worse was that the population of Union during that time was not in support of the incumbent Labor Party. Not being a constituent added only fuel to an already escalating flame; as a result, the wrought of the Cato Administration was upon them. With a striving Tourist Industry, Union Island could have single handedly shouldered all of its financial responsibilities and more, yet the island was still immersed in poverty. It was the expectation of the residents that a fraction of the island's income would be spent for the development of its infrastructure. Unfortunately, that was not in the agenda of the government. The people of Union Island now discontented and resentful of being marginalized used terms such as "Weather Green, and Guava Crop" to describe their economic hardship. The frustration of the people grew to an alarming height until one Friday morning; December 7th, 1979 a contingent of young men under the leadership of Lenox (Bomba) Charles staged a rebellion against the iniquitous state. They used paint to stencil the streets of Ashton with captions such as "Free Union Island" & "Union Island is for Unionites." These messages, which express strong sentimental disgust among the people, remained in the streets for quite some years later.

The quest was for Union Island to be totally separated from the tentacles of St. Vincent, by ushering in its own government. The Royal Police force of St. Vincent and the Grenadines was quickly deployed to shores of Union Island. The revolt that started early that morning with the sound of dynamites and gunshots came to a screeching halt later that day. There was but one casualty unrelated. To restore law and order in Union Island, a curfew was immediately imposed on the entire state. Understandably, the prime minister of that day, Sir Milton Cato, still frightened by the existing hostile atmosphere in the neighboring island of Grenada (Grenadian Revolution) immediately invited the help of the Barbadian troops from Tom Adams' administration out of Barbados. Approximately seven days later they were on the soil of Union Island. The troop remained there for approximately one month before returning to Barbados. Fortunately there were no casualties.

BASIN POND (BASKET)

The name "Basin" was supplanted by the name "Basket" over a century ago. This pond attained that name because of its inability to retain water. "It can leak like a basket sometimes; before you know it, it is dry again," said the late Henry Stewart of Campbell. The caption posted on the board nearby said the following:

This pond is part of the most extensive complex of the eighteenth-century ruins on Union Island. Jean Augier, one of the island's first French settlers, built it sometime around 1760 when he landed on the island. Basin, which is considered one of the largest of the island's ponds, stored and provided water for the plantation slaves. It was entirely paved with local stones and cemented with heated coral and conch shells. After emancipation in 1834, Basin Pond continued to be a main source of water for the local people.

The caption went to say, "Up until the 1950s, it was still used for washing and 'watering' animals."

The last sentence of the above paragraph is not only misleading but also inaccurate; the residents of Ashton Village, and to a greater extent, Campbell, have used this pond for watering animals up until the 1980s. During the entire decade of the 70s, many residents did their laundry at Basket Pond. Currently, this pond is intact, just in need of some cleaning to remove shrubs and dirt that have been accumulating at its base, the result of many years without proper maintenance.

"Basket" is an age-old name known by everyone on Union Island. Yet the name "Basket" was not mentioned once on this notice board that tells the history of the pond. Now this may sound like a trivial issue, but knowing the proper name is necessary for the preservation of the island's history as it continues to evolve. Residents ought not to be cavalier, innocent, or ignorant regarding what the preservation of the island's history, legacy, and heritage means. In bringing this to light, every citizen of Union Island should be exhorted to be vigilant in keeping the island's history alive and intact. To partially paraphrase the current Prime Minister, Dr. Ralph Gonzalves, every square inch of Union Island's his-story and her-story is it's history.

Basket, despite its long history of usefulness, has been tainted by one very unpleasant moment, which to this day continues to be more pronounced at this historical landmark than its sheer purpose and usefulness. Although this unfortunate event transpired more than sixty years ago, it is still vivid in the minds and hearts of some of the residents.

During the rainy months of the year 1950, two young sisters (Patient, age 10, and Agatha, age 11), accompanied by their friend, Zennie, age 10, were about to leave for the pasture of Ms. Irene, where their animals were reared. Their younger sister Elitha, age 3, had wanted to accompany them on their journey, but they were not interested in having her company that morning. Agatha put her wide straw hat on, and she and the two other girls journeyed on foot all the way through Campbell road to the dense vegetation of Ms. Irene's. On reaching Basket Pond, they saw two people on the opposite side washing clothes. They appeared to be wrapped up in the chore and were oblivious of their surroundings. Zennie left the two sisters to take care of her animals that were tied at her mother's plot of land situated a few hundred meters away. Patient and Agatha were fond of sailing boats, and they seized the opportunity to sail their small coconut boats at the pond. They sailed their boats from one end and retrieved them at the other. Racing coconut boats at Basket was something many youngsters had been doing for years. In fact, this art was done almost every day, especially when the pond was filled with water, which was from June to October.

Now Basket Pond was filled with water, and the girls were anxiously racing their boats in the calm of the morning. A light breeze on the grape leaf was all that was needed to make the boats accelerate to the other side of the pond. The girls loved doing it.

Meanwhile, approximately twenty-five minutes had passed, and Zennie, who had left the two sisters earlier, had finished her chore and headed back in the direction of the pond. Immediately, she saw a straw hat floating aimlessly on the water. Something seemed awry; she thought as she observed a small crowd gathered around the pond frantically looking everywhere. Instantly, she went to investigate and observed that the hat belonged to her friend Agatha. She also observed a long stick floating alongside the hat. Her two young friends were nowhere to be found. Zennie shouted the names of both girls several times, and there was a brief search of the nearby area, but all efforts made that morning turned up empty. Suspecting that something had gone tragically wrong, the small group frantically yelled out for help. The alarm was so intense that it drew the attention of others in the vicinity that had been taking care of their animals. Everyone gathered around the pond, looking for any sign of life. Others left the scene terrible troubled but headed for their respective homes nonetheless.

Meanwhile, at Ashton Village, Ms. Siderlyn, the mother of the two sisters, was quite uneasy. She had expected to see her daughters back at home about an hour earlier. Quickly she placed her slippers on her feet and started off for the pastures of Ms. Irene. On her way, she fetched a whip, intending to give them a physical reminder on their behinds to return home more quickly. (And she would have made use of her whip no matter where she met those girls on their way back home.) But before she got anywhere close to Ms. Irene's, she was greeted by the sad news that her daughters were missing and may have drowned at Basket Pond. Unable to contain herself, the dejected mother wept the entire journey to Basket Pond, where onlookers consoled her.

It is conjectured that a breeze may have blown Agatha's hat into the pond. Anxious to retrieve her hat, she quickly fetched a long stick and stretched over the pond to reach it. The light object instead sailed further into the pond. She then stepped into the water in another effort to retrieve her hat and lost her footing on a slippery stone. She fell a couple of feet further and immediately began to panic. Frantically, she tried in vain to regain her footing and keep her head above the water's surface. Her younger sister, Patient, seeing that her sister was in distress, immediately sprang to her rescue. Patient grabbed the same stick and handed it to her struggling sister so that she could get a grip and be pulled out of danger. That turned out to be hazardous as Agatha's pull on the stick was so forceful that Patient instantly lost her footing and fell into the water as well, where they both perished.

No one in the vicinity saw what had happened; hence, no one could help them. And because these two young females could not swim, they slowly sank to the bottom of the pond, where they unfortunately lost their lives. A local diver named Casey Black hoisted them from their watery grave that same day. They both were buried at the same grave at Ashton Cemetery later that day. Shortly after that, Mr. Casey Black suffered a stroke and was unable to function effectively or do regular activities for the remainder of his life.

It was a horrendous day, not just for the parents but also for the community as a whole. Many, many years later, kids were severely warned to exhibit care when extracting water from the eternally useful Basket. Stephen, a son of Ms. Siderlyn, who was born many years after the tragedy, said: "Boy, I couldn't even pass too close to Basket and make my mother know about it. You know how much licks I get just for being at the pond with my friend?"

Unfortunately, Basket Pond is remembered mainly because of the two girls that lost their lives rather than it's many years of conveying water for the residents of Ashton.

◆◆◆□*Chapter Ten*

BASKETBALL

In the early 1970s, basketball made its way to Union Island thanks to our native son, Lennox (Bomba) Charles, a visionary with profound love for his country. Though played seasonally, basketball attracts regional attention from countries such as St. Lucia, Grenada, and teams from the mainland. They all come to Union Island to compete at the annual basketball tournaments during Easterval. Given the dearth of adequate sporting facilities, this small island has been able to breed some relatively fine basketball players. Though opportunities for continuing progress seem distant, that does not deter our youngsters. Their affinity for the sport seems to supersede all obstacles and challenges.

The undeterred propensity for the sport, coupled with the natural talent of these fledglings has enabled them to stand out. They feel secluded in this almost unknown archipelago of the Caribbean Sea. This extraordinary talent was present in Glenroy Ambrose, Aldrick Stowe, Adonol Foyle, and so on. We were, and still are, disadvantaged to the point that accepting defeat becomes the inevitable only because there are no alternatives. But while pertinacity remains an integral part of success in the hearts and minds of our youngsters, age has been their fiercest enemy. Their voices are often echoed unheeded. "If I'd only had the opportunity, I would have..." they say. That brings us to the highest achiever, Adonol Foyle.

Adonol Foyle

Adonol Foyle is a major success we all are proud of. He was born in our neighboring cay of Canouan on March 9, 1975, and attended the Union Island Secondary because it was the only secondary school of the Southerly Grenadines constituency. Many other students from the islands of Mayreau and Canouan also attended it.

Although Adonol Foyle did not have prior knowledge of the sport, he had tremendous talent and later harnessed it. Standing at six feet tall, he was able to ascend to the highest echelon of the basketball establishment. The Golden State Warriors of NBA drafted him in 1997; there he played ten seasons as a center guard until the team bought out his contract on August 13, 2007. At such time, Mr. Foyle was deemed the longest-tenured player. He was also a player at Orlando Magic and a member of the National Basketball Players Association Executive Committee.

In 2005, Foyle founded the Kerosene Lamp Foundation, which serves children in St. Vincent and the Grenadines.

IS THIS LAND YOUR LAND?

Although the enactment of the possessory title act (Act 38 of 2004) of St. Vincent & the Grenadines was intended to benefit the nation as a whole, it surely has proven to be a disadvantage to many landowners in recent years. The principal reason for the stipulation of this act is simple -it allowed a person to own property that belonged to his forefathers, or that he had occupied in good faith for many years. Today, newspapers are inundated on a weekly basis with applications from people seeking to attain deeds via the possessory act. Among them are the opportunists who seize every chance to be the owner of another man's properties.

A long time ago in Union Island, the communal lifestyle and customs enabled people to buy lands without any form of written documentation. Word-of-mouth was all that was needed because people trust each other. Word-of- mouth had clout, and hence was the final authority. However, this has proven to be an impediment in recent years because many of the owners are unable to provide deeds for the lands that they had bought. Many of the ancestors died without having the palest idea that multiple problems would result from those verbal contracts that were once valid and binding. With no deed made out for a portion of land bought during those earlier years, these owners cannot transfer ownership of their lands to their offspring because there are no legal documentations that allow them to do so. Instead, these offspring can only obtain these inherited lands through a lengthy process of administration.

With the above being a quandary-one that bolstered lawmakers to enact a system whereby some form of administration could be initiated (Act 38 of 2004). This permits a person to make a declaration about having a property in his or her possession for twelve or more years. As a result, it enabled some plots of lands to have deeds for the first time. But there were many unoccupied lands whose taxes haven't been paid for many years. This gives many intruders the opportunity to pilfered land that they had no ties to. They have falsely declared that they had occupied those lands for more that twelve years as satisfactory to the possessory title act (Act 38 of 2004). Also, professionals who are privy to the law, they too took advantage of the situation to acquire lands for themselves rather than apprising some of the less fortunate who has legitimate family ties to those lands.

The application process begins with a surveyed plan of the land that must be no older than two years, and must bear the applicant's name. All landowners whose lands border the property in question must be properly informed; hence, a bailiff must be employed for this purpose. Following that is the affidavits of service that must be filed on time showing total compliance. Two postings of the application must be done on a newspaper over a three-months period. Then followed by the inevitable—the court hearing, which should bring closure in a short period of time. But if the application is contested it can result in a protracted hearing. But after the entire process, the court should be able to present the possessory title to the worthy person.

Is the application process followed as required by the law of the land? The answer is a resounding no! The landowners whose lands border the properties are never informed until they realized that they have new neighbors. At such time, it might be just to late. Someone, somewhere has lost a property.

Regardless of where these legitimate landowners reside; the burden of responsibility still lies on them to ensure that their properties are not listed in these newspapers and are later taken over by unscrupulous persons. It is because of the mass exodus of the younger generation who has been seeking employment abroad why lands remained under the stewardship of their parents and relatives. Unfortunately, when their parents and relatives die, many properties are left abandoned. Regrettably, this has allowed many opportunistic land predators to relieve lands from those who should rightfully inherit them. It is the opinion of many that this unethical practice should come to a screeching halt.

It is important to note that this dastardly act of pilfering private lands in Union Island remains a public crime and not simply a private wrong; a wrong that should be punishable by a considerable amount of time spent behind bars.

Dr. Kendall Stewart

Dr. Kendall B. Stewart

Earlier in this book, mention was made of migrants who have sought other frontiers for greater employment opportunities and educational advancement. Among the many, here is the success story of one of Union Island's native son, Dr. Kendall Basil Stewart.

Dr. Kendall Stewart is the grandnephew of Captain Hugh Mulzac. Deemed the Honorable Kendall Stewart for the vast contributions he has made, in the life of New Yorkers in the New York metropolitan area, his name, life, and legacy are permanently etched into the cornerstone of the history of New York. He is an esteemed visionary with fervent passion in humanism. His motto is: "To hear him is to help him, to help him is to know him, to know him is to love him, to love him is to see his vision of community development and empowerment."

Dr. Kendall Stewart was born in Ashton, Union Island. He is the son of the late Solomon and Millicent Stewart of Ashton, Union Island. Like this author, he is the fourth-generation of the esteemed Mr. William McDowell and his wife, Mrs. Louisiana Stewart nee Wilson. They are the root and sole ancestors of Union Island's entire Stewart family, which was the largest segment of the island's population.

The former state committeeman of the 58th Assembly District and member of the Kings County State Democratic Committee in Brooklyn, New York, Kendall Stewart served on the city council for eight years, held membership in many social and educational groups, and was the recipient of countless awards. Board certified in podiatric surgery he is a member of the Podiatric Medical Association, American Podiatric Circulatory Society, and American Institute of Foot Medicine, and he is a medical panel member of Local 1199 and many other local organizations.

From the Ashton primary school on Union Island, Kendall Stewart migrated to St. Vincent to better his education. Then later, he traveled to Trinidad, West Indies, where he attended the Caribbean Union College. Several years later, he graduated. His penchant for a better life coupled with his passion for learning propelled him to migrate to the United States, where he became a graduate of Albert Merrill School of Computer Science and earned his Bachelor of Science degree from City College of New York. From there he went on to earn his doctoral degree in podiatric medicine from New York City College of Podiatric Medicine.

At his office at 4016 Church Avenue, this is what Dr. Kendall Stewart had to say: "When I was a boy, my parents told me that my hands were very important, and whatever I touched turns to gold."

This Midas-like philosophy that this humanitarian possesses is what bolstered him and gave him that extra impetus to take on all of life's challenges with renewed celerity.

Epilogue

I have come to the point where I must close this book. My passion tells me to continue writing, but I am quite aware that there will always be another day to write another story. I have labeled this book part 1, for there is much more that I will like to share in part 2. During my literary journey, on Union Island Then & Now, my greatest motivation was to convey successfully what is pent up in me for almost my entire life. Because of this, I spent sleepless nights on my computer pecking away at the keyboard. My hope was to be exhausted of the copious information that saturates my brain. I later coined the phrase: *"While many are comfortably asleep, I am wide-awake and tediously at work."*

On some occasions, it appeared that I was living for one reason, and one reason only, and that was to eat sleep and drink-in the history of Union Island. This I did, because it was never made available to be read, not even in the classroom. Well, I did, and this I observed is the existing state of the Now on this still unblemished landmass.

Throughout the entire 20th Century, though various elements in part have contributed to the current state of Union island's culture, the principal underlying part must be ascribed to the ever-present Exodus Factor. With the age of social transformation reaping havoc everywhere, the people of Union Island though without mass institutions of change, are awakening to a new dawn. The once vibrant agricultural sector is now at the mercy of a technologically advanced demographic that assumes the title, "knowledge workers." Today, as the quest for academic advancements, becomes even greater, so too does the quest to venture abroad to pursue a better life. This, however, has resulted in a mass exodus of natives to several developed countries to satisfy those needs.

History has taught us enough about the formally

ubiquitous cotton crop that literally began its declination during the mid 19th Century. Later it has given way to the corn/pea crops during the turn of the 20th Century. Although the latter are currently at its lowest, no significant crop has supplanted them thus far. Hence, the subsistent factor that was considerably dominant for the better part of the 20th Century is now archaic as its compatriot - the old bartering system. The absence of exports of the island's resources such as Tamarind, Divi-Divi, sugar apples, crabs, and bi-products of farming and fishing have disappeared over the years. The numerous vessels that have been an integral part of the import/export trade for a period of eight decades have taken a significant nosedive, unfortunately. The Fishing industry too is impact negatively since those principal fishermen have transitioned to the ancestors. Again the Exodus Factor is partially to be blamed for this.

The Maroon, Vessel Launching, Maypole dance, Fisherman's Party, Harvest, Regatta, Woman's Police Day, Dancing of the Cake & Flag of the traditional marriage, and many other customary practices over the past 50 years have practically gone by the wayside resulting in a declination of the island's culture and some of its invaluable virtues. Nevertheless, the Wake, Lightening Up (All Saints Night) and Christmas Carol serenading is struggling to remain alive. The Easter gala that has evolved into the noted Easterval celebration is currently gaining momentum and has supplanted the age-old communal spirit of Christmas.

Amazingly! A population of 3.5 thousand remained constant, amidst one century of incessant farewells.

Bibliography

Ancestry.co.uk© 2002-2013 Ancestry.com.

Ancestry. Com © 1997-2013 Ancestry.com.

Forward Susan Ph.D. (1997) Emotional Blackmail. Harper Collins Publishers, Inc., USA.

King James Authorized Version. The Holy Bible.

Lennox Charles (1976) The Daylight Magazine.

Morse. (1778) Report on the Grenadines to Lord Mac Carthney.

Mulzac H. N. (1963). A star to Steer by. International Publishers, co., Inc. USA.

Nichols H. Dr. (1891) Diary of a trip through Grenada, the Grenadines and St. Vincent.

Scrubb-Kirby, Cleo (1975) The Unionite Magazine.

St. Vincent Gazette (Government).

About the Author

Born on Union Island, a young Josiah only three months old was taken to Trinidad, an island where his parents were able to get work to provide food for three young children. Already a student of the Piccadilly Government School, Port-of-Spain, Josiah now six years of age, was brought back to the land of his birth. To him, Union Island was a new world; a place that he instantly fell in love with, for it represented freedom -the kind that he has never experienced anywhere else. Even today! Amazingly, he immersed himself fully into the island's lifestyle and quietly drank his full of its dialect, customs, mores, and folkways. He reared goats, sheep, cattle, and pigs on almost every pasture of Campbell. Fully engrossed into the garden that provided plentifully, he played a significant role there too.

He attended both primary schools of Ashton, and in 1972, he was enrolled into the Union Island Junior Secondary School. This school was timely built to elevate the then horrific educational level that existed for a long time. Despite attaining favorable grades throughout his school life, assimilating into the educational system of that day was exceedingly challenging.

Young, vibrant, energetic, and strong, a teenaged Josiah, left Union Island to perpetuate "the Exodus Factor," that had already been an integral part of Union island's culture. Fortunately he was already impacted sturdily by the island's culture and an unquenchable desire to excel -an asset that he held on to tenaciously. In his quest to excel on foreign soils, he learned firsthand that the importance of food, clothes, and shelter superseded everything else -Maslow Hierarchy of Needs.

Also in those adverse environments where the status of residence may be unfriendly, the ability to advance is often met with fierce sustained challenges. As a result, countless educational dreams and aspirations were reluctantly sidelined. He indicated that this plight is not exclusive to himself, but an experience that most Caribbean people from all walks of life has endured on frontiers thousands of miles away from their true habitats. "With transformation, my life has just begun," he said, "and as Caribbean people we all have a testimony of a similar nature to share." He continued, "For me, perseverance is the key, but one's character is the litmus test."

THE ANCESTORS

Below are the names of the ancestors of Union Island: The mothers, fathers, aunts, uncles, sisters, brothers, grandmothers, grandfathers, great grandmothers, great grandfathers and cousins. 90% of which the author have known personally, the other 10%, he have seen and may have spoken with at least once.

This journey starts from the district of Campbell, Ashton, and has ascended to all other localities on the island. If by chance the author have missed or failed to include anyone's name, it is only by error. Nevertheless, Unionites must take into consideration that none of their beloved deceased have transition before the year 1967. Peruse carefully with a sense of wistfulness.

Frederick Hempseed, (Whiteman Fred), Presaul Ambrose (Presey), Patient & Bertram Stewart (Big City), Garfield Stewart (Daddy Gaf), Simeon Stewart (Daddy Stroad), Henry Stewart (Soft walks), Mc Kay John, Blossom & Adrian (Burn man, Mammam Muey) Simmons, Elmina & Gilbert Cox, Cynthia and Ewirth Cox, Janie & Goldstein Alexander, Meldon & Emelda John, Verna & Sylvan Hutchinson, Fred & Zena John, Emelda & Milton John, Oscar John, Iola & Norris (Zuggy) Harvey, Anella & Garnet Stewart, Elma & Russell Wilson (Russ), Fegina & Gordon Hutchinson, Mary and Mano Hutchinson, Faith Ambrose, Mavis Ambrose, Inez & Ewing Alexander, Audley Alexander (Sugar in the boots) Dora Campbell (One hand Dora), Jestina Alexander (Jesso), Benita Thomas, William Thomas, May John, Muriel Hutchinson, Pricilla John (Porcho), Eris Samuel, Incoman & Millicent Stewart, Gifted Wilson, Uncle Bus, Elizabeth Simmons (Liz) Tantoo Wilson, David John (Gayman, Lally), Maudlin Polson, Siderlyn Wilson, Purgin Wilson, Ina & Son Allot, Evelyn & Caser Room, Harriet & Theopolis Longdon, Henny & Theophilus Regis (Toffee), Mattie Thomas, Anesta Harvey, Euthrice Warner, Veda & Thomas Coy, Helena & Joseph William, Izolyn Bibby, Faithful Bibby (Jitterbug), Joseph Roberson (Jiggery), Luther Bibby (Bronson), Agatha & Harold Dennis (Jap) Safety Hypolite, Mie (Ta Mie) & Mc Cauley Vesprey, Leah & Robert Wilson (Tojo), Pricilla

(Mom, Look sin) & Wilton Wilson (Wash brain), Faith Coban, Dolly & James Selby, Shuvvy Mitchell (Poo-Pa), Mona Jones (Ma Mone), Anella Harvey, Mildred & Festus Hutchinson (Esso), Lena and Royal Noel, Tyrell Harvey (City), Federica & Shem Room, Beatrice Samuel (Day-tay), Iris & Persival John (Bus), Bentley Stewart, Alice Scrub & Allan Scrub (Bah Allan), Sara Hutchinson (Miss Tony), Medford Blencoe, Ritiann & Claude Scrub, Henrietta Ambrose, Augustine Cox, Mary & Wycliffe Hutchinson, Maybe Ambrose (Tan-Tan), Gussy Hutchinson, Lettuce & Pentland Selby (Ah-who-whay), Elizabeth Cox (Dee-Dee), Terrence Scrub (Blow Way), Peter Wilson (father priece), Rosetta Scrub, Clyde Selby (Ah-who-whay), Catharine Regis, Eurina Ambrose (Ta - hn), Bernadette Noel, Gladys Simmons, Samuel Regis (Sweet Rose), Lucy & Wilfred Daniel (Santas), Viola & Joseph Alexander (Uncle Joe), Samuel Saxon, Rubina & Carlton Lucas, Patient Wilson (Ma-phish), Julie Wilson, Mc Neal Cox, Icy & Leacock John, Hudson Mulzac (Cayenne Waist), Clem Stewart, Theopolis Stewart, Joycelyn Quashie, Una & Joseph Hutchinson, Alcina & Lawrence Wilson (Larry), Etty Scrub (Tettie), Ethneil Mitchell, Arabella Cyrus (Brown Best), Isabella Harvey (Bella), Conscience Scrub, Priscilla & Leo Gellizeau, Civil Ackie, Jane Ann Daniel (Tan Jane), Lemuel Ambrose (Lem), Canny Ambrose, (Brother Can), Amos Stewart, Mercy & Isaac Hutchinson, Fred Hutchinson, Jonah Stewart, Elaine Simmons (Ta Lain), Flora Ambrose, Princess Alexander, Alfred Cox, Johnson Thomas (JT), Preston Ramage (Caber), Venetta & Almond Mitchell (Cat balloon), Patricia & Ozias Paul, Ada Scrubb, Millicent Alexis, Lydian & Conrad Ramage, Johnnie Joseph, Caroline & Gransul Joseph (Lab), Julia Joseph (Momma), Herbert Thomas (Thomas), Aaron Douglas, (Doug), Elaine Wells (Mother Lyn), Lucita Joseph, Millicent & Solomon Stewart (Ball afire) Stella & Fen Badnock, Denzil Stewart, Percival Thomas (Brother Tom), Florence Forde, Amelia Scrub (Ms. Popo), Nathaniel Stewart, Joseph & Baby Collis, Rosalyn Jones, Ruthven Alexander, Ms. Lyn Room, Tyrell Wilson, Sonny Wilson, Masoon Wilson (Tanty Ma), Esther & Theopholus James, Linda & Jerrus Stewart, Rebecca Noel (Faithful) & Mc Clarence Noel, Elbert Jones (Chammer), Ellen & Jonathan Alexander (Lixy), William Stewart (William Toast), Claude Ambrose, Fluorine Charles, George & Princess Samuel, Lenie Joseph (Dema, Aunty Mearl), Victoria Hutchinson (Miss Vic), Florence Wilson, Boysie Scrubb, Agatha Simmons, Rosa & Pablo Scrubb, Mildred Simeon, George Hutchinson (King George), Mary Stewart (Mary Tall away) & Norbert Stewart, Ms. Tensy, Antho & Augustin Ramage, Eny & Efford Joseph, Mary Edwards,

Winston Douglas (Sky-Lay), Mary Stewart (Ce Mary), Fena, Mrs. Daphne Ackie, Ms. Brownie, Advira Adams, Wap-Wap Stewart, Dogma Mulzac, Cleve Mulrain, Ms. Mo & Kent Hutchinson, Ony Scrubb, Miriam James, Willimina Adams, Essie Stewart & Charles Jones, Avis Mills & Casey Abraham, Maybe & George Clouden, Margaret Ovid, Ifield Pope, Mariah Clouden, Edmond John, James Stewart, Mc Kay (Brother Mc Kie), Dora (Martha) & James Stewart (Chiquita), Suzanna Hall, Lillian Robinson & Ellie Andrew (Woopsin), Corn-do-doo, Ernest Mc Tair, Amuthel & Conrad Adams, Princess & Milford Mc Intosh, Benjamin Adams, Rosanna Charles, Donna Dallas, Virginia & Sylvester Alexander (Sylves) Morgan Snagg, Rachel, Noreen Alexander, Carolyn Roache (Tillix), Janey Stewart, Alston Charles, Janey Roache, Violet & Jonathan Roache, Ezekiel Roache, Peter Alexander, James Cudjoe, Nurse Celina Clouden, Olive Clowden, Civil & Abraham Snagg (Bram), Victoria Hypolite (Tanty Vic), Nathanial Alexander (Natty), Vincent Brown(Biggest), Crystal Clouden, Vileria McTair, Angelic Saxon, Baby, John Roache, Branford Saxon & Loquisha, David James, Lorna John, Ceretha, Walton Bubb.

There are quite a bit of names here. Although the names of many ancestors are missing from both villages, a better job was done with the ancestors of Ashton than those of Clifton.

CPSIA information can be obtained
at www.ICGtesting.com
Printed in the USA
LVOW12s1716120516

487975LV00001B/55/P